The Akkadian Empire

An Enthralling Overview of the Rise and Fall of the Akkadians

Free limited time bonus

Stop for a moment. We have a free bonus set up for you. The problem is this: we forget 90% of everything that we read after 7 days. Crazy fact, right? Here's the solution: we've created a printable, 1-page pdf summary for this book that you're reading now. All you have to do to get your free pdf summary is to go to the following website: **https://livetolearn.lpages.co/enthrallinghistory/**

Once you do, it will be intuitive. Enjoy, and thank you!

We forget 90% of everything that we've read in 7 days...

Get the free printable pdf summary of the book you've read AND much, much more... shhhh...

Enter Your Most Frequently Used Email to Get Started

DOWNLOAD FREE PDF SUMMARY

© Enthralling History

Contents

Introduction

Akki, the gardener, stretched his sun-bronzed arms and scowled at the rows of barley yet to be watered. He resolutely plodded to the river with two buckets. The sun sparkled on the river's surface, momentarily blinding Akki as he lowered one of the buckets into the water. Thump! What did the bucket hit? There! Bumping against the shore was a covered basket.

How curious! Setting the bucket aside, Akki squatted down and lifted the basket out of the water. It seemed heavy. What was inside? He noted the bitumen covering the basket; someone wanted it to be waterproof. But why? Carefully, he unlatched the top and looked inside. Something was moving under the small blanket! Akki jumped back for a moment, then heard a whimpering sound. He carefully pulled aside the blanket to find a newborn infant, whose sudden exposure to the bright sun made him horrifically wail.

"There, there, little one," he cooed. "You're all right. You're safe now." As if in a dream, Akki lifted the baby to his shoulder and began walking across the fields, never realizing he held the first king of the world's first empire.

If you mentioned the Akkadian Empire to a group of people, chances are you'd get some quizzical looks or blank stares. Most people have never heard of the world's first multi-national empire with a powerful, centralized government. Preceding the Babylonian, Assyrian, Egyptian, Chinese, and Indian empires by centuries, the Akkadian Empire rose to power in 2334 BCE to rule all of ancient Mesopotamia—and beyond!

Was there anything approaching an empire before the Akkadian Empire? In southern Mesopotamia, Sumer's city-states formed several mini-empires, with one city's king exercising "kingship" over other cities in the region. However, these were more like small countries, covering less than one hundred square miles. Everyone shared the same culture, spoke the same language, and prayed to the same gods. By contrast, the Akkadian Empire encompassed multiple ethnicities and languages: Sumerian, Akkadian, Elamite, Syrian, Canaanite, and more. At its zenith, the empire stretched from the Mediterranean Sea to the Persian Gulf, including Mesopotamia, Elam, Anatolia, Syria, Lebanon, and Canaan.

This history of the Akkadian Empire reveals many captivating mysteries of this vast realm. What civilizations existed in Mesopotamia before Akkad gained supremacy? What were the Akkadians' origins? How did they gain sovereignty over other cultures and form their vast power network? What myths drove the Akkadian culture, and what religion did they follow? How did their art and culture reflect their belief system? Who were their most famous rulers, and what made them exceptional? What were the distinctive features of their military and warfare strategies? What was everyday life like in the Akkadian Empire? Why did the Akkadian Empire collapse? How did the Akkadian culture continue to influence future Mesopotamian dynasties? This book will answer these questions and many more.

You might be wondering how this book is different from other Akkadian Empire histories. For one thing, few authors have written a comprehensive overview of this topic since the renowned archaeologist Leonard W. King published *A History of Sumer and*

Akkad in 1910. Some generalized histories of Mesopotamia contain a chapter or two on the Akkadian Empire, but few are devoted solely to the Akkadian Empire.

Of the handful of books written on Akkad, most focus on specific aspects, such as Benjamin R. Foster's fascinating study of Sargonic and pre-Sargonic cuneiform texts, Melissa Eppihimer's enchanting overview of the Akkadian artistic legacy, and Alan Lenzi's enlightening introduction to Akkadian literature. This book presents a comprehensive, authoritative history drawing from the scholarly research of King, Foster, Eppihimer, Lenzi, and other Mesopotamian specialists to deliver the most recent archaeological and cultural studies. This broad overview endeavors to bring Sargon the Great and his enthralling Akkadian Empire to life in an engaging, easy-to-understand format.

Exploring past civilizations is enriching and empowering. When we understand how cultures developed, what made them extraordinary, and what led to their downfalls, we have a broader understanding of our world today. Yesterday's cultures inform our worldview and our belief systems. Comprehensive knowledge of history gives us a deeper understanding of our global state of affairs. Past victories inspire and motivate us, and past failures warn us what not to do.

Examining the spectacular rise and fall of the world's first true empire is invigorating. It's almost overwhelming to imagine how Sargon, a humble gardener, seemingly arose from nothing to conquer and rule the land between the Euphrates and Tigris Rivers (today's Iraq). Then he and his descendants pressed on to dominate the ancient territories of present-day Iran, Turkey, Syria, Lebanon, Syria, Canaan, and Oman. A keen understanding of ancient Mesopotamia gives insight into today's rich Middle Eastern cultures and turbulent political landscape.

Join us as we explore the influence of the Ubaid and Sumerian cultures that preceded the Akkadian civilization, the explosion of change wrought by the Akkadian Empire, how the empire operated, and how it continued to influence events and culture in the Middle East.

Chapter 1: The Ubaid Period

Who were the early people in southern Mesopotamia, with their lizard-lady figurines and entrancing pottery? How did they live, and what did they accomplish in the mysterious millennia before writing began? Although they formed the first true empire, the Akkadians were not the first civilization in Mesopotamia; in fact, they were relative newcomers to the scene. Before the Akkadians arrived, the Sumerians lived in central and southern Mesopotamia, sharing a common history and culture since around 3800 BCE, which later intertwined with the Akkadian culture. Before the Sumerians, although it overlaps a bit, the mysterious Ubaid civilization and several other prehistoric cultures farmed and herded livestock in Mesopotamia.

What do we know about these prehistoric cultures? By 5500 BCE, in the mid-Neolithic period, the Hassuna, Samarra, and Halaf cultures emerged in northern Mesopotamia, living in agricultural villages with baked-clay homes and circular domed temples. The Samarra culture was in central-northern Mesopotamia, where scholars believe Akkad was located. The Hassuna culture was immediately north of Samarra, and the Halaf culture was to the west. Although their distinctive pottery set them apart, these three civilizations overlapped and intermingled.

How advanced were these civilizations? All three prehistoric cultures used axes, sickles, grinding stones, baking ovens, and simple plows. They had stamp seals, which were about one inch in diameter, with a picture carved into stone that they pressed into soft clay as a sort of signature. They made cream-slip pottery painted with reddish linear designs. They grew emmer wheat, barley, and flax, and they herded sheep, goats, and cattle.

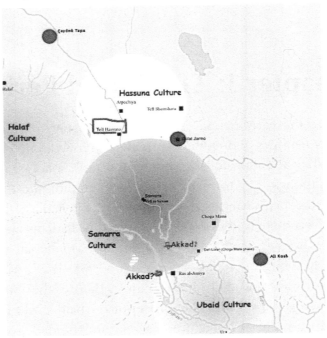

This map shows the prehistoric cultures' locations in ancient Mesopotamia prior to the Sumerian civilization and Akkadian Empire. Two possible sites of Akkad are noted in the lower map, and Tell Hassuna is circled in the upper map.

In northern Iraq in 1942, a farmer was plowing the soil to plant lentils on a hill covered with wildflowers when he found some pottery shards. After closer inspection, archaeologist Sayid Fu'ād

Safar determined that this hill, which was twenty-two miles southwest of today's Mosul, was actually a tell, which he named *Tell Hassuna*. A "tell" is an artificial hill or mound of accumulated, stratified debris from buildings, garbage, tombs, vegetation, and earth left by ancient generations of people who once lived there. Over the centuries—or over the millennia, in this case—buildings crumble, and nature slowly reclaims the area. In the desert and semi-arid regions like Iraq, blowing sand usually covers the tells until it's hard to distinguish them from natural land formations. In fact, the Akkadian Empire's capital of Agade (Akkad) still lies buried under the sand. No one knows quite where it is.

What did the archaeological exploration of the site reveal? Tell Hassuna and other similar tells provide valuable information about the preexisting Hassuna, Samarra, and Halaf civilizations in what would later be the Akkadian Empire region. Although the tell was in the Hassuna region, many Samarra and Halaf pottery artifacts were in the upper layers, indicating that all three cultures coexisted in the area or traded with each other. Since these cultures were preliterate, we rely on archaeological excavations for clues about these ancient civilizations.

Safar teamed up with Seton Lloyd, President of the British School of Archaeology in Iraq, to explore Tell Hassuna. Lloyd and Safar initially thought the pottery was more recent and were excited to discover they were wrong! The more they excavated, the older the artifacts they were unearthing. The Tell Hassuna's lowest and oldest level—twenty-two feet down—dated to the Neolithic Era.[1] The oldest layer appeared to be remnants of hunter/gatherers or possibly herders who used stone tools and made thick, coarse pottery. Safar and Lloyd found hearths or fire pits but no houses. They did find woven reed matting that might have been used as a covering for

---

[1] Seton Lloyd, Fuad Safar, and Robert J. Braidwood, "Tell Hassuna Excavations by the Iraq Government Directorate General of Antiquities in 1943 and 1944," *Journal of Near Eastern Studies* 4, no. 4 (1945): 255–89. http://www.jstor.org/stable/542914.

huts, except they didn't find any post holes or anything hinting at a support structure. Perhaps the reed matting was the remnants of baskets or sleeping mats. These Neolithic people were either tent dwellers, like today's Bedouins, or used little or no shelter at all.

Lloyd's team uncovered obsidian lanceheads and slingshot ammunition for hunting. They found stone-headed axes, which they believed may have been used to break the ground for simple farming. The archaeologists were intrigued to find a skeleton between two cooking hearths. They wondered if the person had been buried in a shallow grave or if he or she died in an abandoned settlement.

This Hassuna redware bowl dates to about 5500 BCE.
https://commons.wikimedia.org/wiki/File:Hassuna_redware_bow
l.jpg

The middle layer was the Hassuna culture (5500–3800 BCE). They lived in adobe houses. At first, these were crudely constructed, one-room dwellings, but they later had several rooms. The Hassuna pottery was painted and more sophisticated than the Neolithic culture. The Hassuna culture used stone mortars and barrel-shaped clay ovens with one opening. They would light a fire inside to heat the oven, then put out the fire, sweep out the ashes, and put in the bread dough. The clay walls of the oven stayed hot long enough for the bread to bake. Near the ovens were clay disks; the archaeologists theorized these were "potboilers." The Hassuna would put them into the oven for a while, and when they were hot, they would drop them into a pot of water to heat them up.

In the Hassuna layers, Safar and Lloyd discovered sickle blades of flint and obsidian, and beneath the houses, they found grain bins, leading them to think the Hassuna were grain farmers. Animal bones at the site revealed they also herded cattle, sheep, and goats. The upper Hassuna layer displayed the sophisticated Samarra pottery and many Halaf ceramics, which indicates trade or homogeneity between the neighboring people.

Archaeologists found this circa 5000 BCE bottle-shaped jar painted with a woman's face in the Hassuna layer of Tell Hassuna, representing Samarra culture.
https://commons.wikimedia.org/wiki/File:Neck_of_a_painted_jar_from_Tell _Hassuna,_Iraq,_belonging_to_Samarra_culture._5000_BCE._Iraq_Museu m.jpg

They found the skeletal remains of infants buried in pottery jars under the houses and one complete skeleton of an older child or small adult curled into the fetal position in what appeared to be part of a room in a house sealed off by stone. Interestingly, the Assyrians, whose culture emerged in the same region about one thousand years later, also followed this custom of burying loved ones under or within their homes.

The upper layers contained remnants of Ubaid-style pottery and some artifacts from the late Ubaid and Akkadian-Assyrian cultures. The buildings in these layers were built of stone. Safar and Lloyd found no copper in any of the levels, but they did find antimony and malachite, which would have been used to make kohl eye makeup. They unearthed more adult human skeletons buried in an orderly fashion. Two skeletons, however, were flung helter-skelter into a pit. Were they the victims of foul play? Were they executed? Mysteries like this leave archaeologists scratching their heads.

The Ubaid culture (5500–3800 BCE) emerged slightly later in central and southern Mesopotamia but continued through the same period as the Halaf, Samarra, and Hassuna cultures. The Sumerian culture would later develop in the Ubaid region, and Akkad probably lay where the prehistoric Samarra and Ubaid cultures connected geographically. The name "Ubaid" derives from *Tell al-'Ubaid*—an archaeological site just west of the ancient city of Ur on what was then the Persian Gulf coast. The Persian Gulf later receded south about 155 miles due to silt deposits from the Euphrates and Tigris Rivers. Another factor for reduced sea levels was global cooling and increased ice packs on the northern and southern poles.

What does archaeology tell us about the Ubaid culture? Ubaidians used adzes (something like an ax), hoes, and knives, and they wove linen and wool, as loom weights and spindle whorls were uncovered. They made bricks to build houses and formed distinctive painted pottery and figurines. Several households shared outdoor clay bread ovens. Occupations included carpenters, farmers, fishermen, herders, potters, and weavers.

Did the Ubaidians establish the world's first city? The Ubaid culture is divided into several periods, which mainly revolve around the changes in pottery. The Ubaid I period centers around the city of Eridu in Mesopotamia's far south. Eridu was a few miles west of Ur and on the Persian Gulf at that time (now its ruins lie in a desert wasteland). Many archaeologists believe Eridu, which was first settled around 5400 BCE by the Ubaidians, is the world's oldest city. However, it didn't achieve true city status until the later Sumerian era, when it grew into a sizeable city covering one hundred acres. In the Ubaid period, it had about four thousand people, making it a large town.

How could the Ubaidians farm in semi-desert conditions? Eridu's people could grow grain despite the hot, arid conditions because the nearby Euphrates River fed Lake Hammar. The Eridu settlement sat on two shores—the Persian Gulf to the south and Lake Hammar to the west—which, at that time, was freshwater (now it's saline). [2] This proximity to the sea and a freshwater lake provided an irrigation source and an abundance of seafood.

---

[2] Carrie Hritz, et al. "Revisiting the Sealands: Report of Preliminary Ground Reconnaissance in the Hammar District, Dhi Qar and Basra Governorates, Iraq," *Iraq* 74 (2012): 37–49. http://www.jstor.org/stable/23349778.

This clay model of a sailboat lay buried in a man's grave in Ubaid-era Eridu. https://www.jstor.org/stable/43072618

The Ubaid culture's access to the Persian Gulf, Lake Hammar, and the Euphrates and Tigris Rivers also led to the use of boats. And not only simple canoes or rafts but sailboats! Archaeologists unearthed clay models of sailboats in the gravesites of Uruk, Eridu, and other Ubaid towns.[3] These early sailboats—the first in the world for which we have archaeological evidence—were simple yet served as a prototype for more sophisticated designs in the future.

The earliest Ubaid people in Eridu lived in reed-thatched huts and enjoyed a wide variety of food. They fished and dug shellfish from the gulf and the lake. They hunted waterfowl, gazelle, and other wild animals, and they herded goats and sheep, which provided milk, meat, and wool. They ate the wild einkorn wheat and later began cultivating it. In the Ubaid I period, they carried water to their fields, but by the mid-Ubaid period, they had learned to dig canals for irrigating larger fields, which created a surplus of grain.

---

[3] E. Douglas Van Buren, "Discoveries at Eridu," *Orientalia* 18, no. 1 (1949): 123–24. http://www.jstor.org/stable/43072618.

As time went by, they built more permanent houses by forming bricks from the wetland mud, which provided better protection from the hot sun. The early mud-brick homes were rectangle-shaped and had several rooms with plastered floors and flat roofs constructed from beams and rushes covered by plaster. Eventually, the town covered about twenty-five acres with approximately four thousand people in an area surrounded by smaller villages.

What was the Ubaid culture's religion? A small one-room temple, first built around 5300 BCE, stood in the town's center. At one end was a sacrificial altar, and at the other end was a niche for a deity image. The question is, who did they worship? Multiple images of a female figure with a reptilian head have been found in Ubaid-era tells in southern Mesopotamia. Were these Ubaidian deities?

This reptilian-headed woman nursing a baby came from Ur, Ubaid Period (4500–4000 BCE). Figures of slim women with lizard-like heads were a common motif in the Ubaid culture.

What were these lizard ladies all about? They were small, only two to six inches tall, with slanted eyes and elongated heads and noses. By comparison, ancient female figurines from the Hassuna,

Samarra, and Halaf cultures were plump, seated ladies with large thighs and pendulous breasts. The Ubaid female statuettes are thin, with flat tummies and smaller breasts; they look somewhat androgynous. A few figurines are male, and some are of indeterminate gender. These figurines were often found in adult human graves but never in children's graves. The Ubaid typically buried their dead resting on their back, with their hands resting on their pelvis, which is how many reptilian figures appeared.[*] Scholars have yet to determine if they had religious significance—yet another head-scratching mystery!

Eridu was consistently inhabited through the end of the Ubaid culture, and it was abandoned around 3800 BCE, perhaps due to the same flooding that struck Ur several miles east. Ur and Uruk were two other prominent towns that emerged in southern Mesopotamia in the Ubaid I period. The Sumerians would later inhabit these two settlements, which grew into large cities dominating Sumer (southern Mesopotamia). Ur was in a strategic position, as it was about twelve miles east of Eridu, where the Euphrates River flowed into the Persian Gulf. Uruk was about forty miles north of Ur on the eastern bank of the Euphrates. Around the time that Ur and Uruk were established, the Ubaid civilization blended with northern Mesopotamia's Halaf culture, forming the Halaf-Ubaid Transitional period.

The Ubaid II period (4800–4500 BCE) is renowned for its striking Hadji Muhammed pottery and the first irrigation agriculture with canal networks. Building the irrigation canals required coordinated and collective work—a historic milestone. During this period, the Ubaid formed extensive trade networks, stretching down the Persian Gulf coast to Bahrain and Oman, west into Arabia, and into the Mediterranean. Since Eridu and Ur were coastal towns

---

[*] R. Carter and Graham Philip, *Beyond the Ubaid: Transformation and Integration in the Late Prehistoric Societies of the Middle East*, Chicago: The Oriental Institute, University of Chicago, 2010, 149-161.

(before the Persian Gulf shrank), they likely used boats to travel along the coast. They also traded with settlements in Turkey and Armenia for obsidian, which is a razor-sharp black volcanic glass used to make arrow and knife blades.

This Hadji Muhammed pottery jar dates to the Ubaid III era, circa 5300-4600 BCE.

The later Ubaid period (4500–3800 BCE) is notable for progress in distinctive ceramics, including stamp seals with designs of birds, snakes, and humans. In 1990, archaeologist Andrew Moore from the Rochester Institute of Technology and British archaeologist Tony Wilkinson discovered pottery kilns in Eridu and Ur that indicated industrial-scale pottery manufacturing took place in these towns in the later Ubaid era.[5]

---

[5] A. M. T. Moore, "Pottery Kiln Sites at al 'Ubaid and Eridu," *Iraq* 64 (2002): 69–77. https://doi.org/10.2307/4200519.

Around 4500 BCE, social stratification emerged in the towns, with larger houses in the town center. Likely, these people had more wealth and probably more power. Also, in the later Ubaid period, distinctions arose in the pottery between the Ubaid settlements of southern Mesopotamia and northern Mesopotamia. In their appraisal of Khanijdal East, a small, late Ubaid settlement in the Jazira plain of northern Iraq, archaeologist Tony Wilkinson and his team noted differences in the shape and decoration of pottery, materials used to make the pottery, and firing techniques.[6] They discovered numerous small clay figurines of sheep and goats; they believed these did not have religious significance but were children's toys. They found one in an infant's grave, along with a rattle.

Ubaid pottery was of superior quality. It was usually a buff color but sometimes yellow, yellow-green, pink, or orange. Firing at an especially hot temperature made it harder and more durable. The pottery fabric (clay characteristics) usually contained rich plant-based temper and occasionally gritty sand. (In pottery making, temper is something mixed with clay that helps prevent cracking and shrinking in the drying and firing process). The Ubaid people generally painted them with black geometric shapes or occasionally floral or animal motifs. Pottery came in all sizes and shapes: pitchers, jars, bowls (both shallow and deep), cooking pots, and cups.

[6] T. J., B. Wilkinson, H. Monahan, and D. J. Tucker, "Khanijdal East: A Small Ubaid Site in Northern Iraq," *Iraq* 58 (1996): 17–50. https://doi.org/10.2307/4200417.

This rounded-bottom Ubaid bowl, circa 5000 BCE, features a yellow-greenish color.

A distinctive Ubaid pottery style of southern Mesopotamia is *Hadji Muhammed*. The potter used a dark-purple color wash over the ceramic, then scraped the vessel into designs to reveal the buff color underneath. Patterns included herringbone, checkerboard, and sinuous curves. This pottery type emerged in the Ubaid I period but is found in later Ubaid periods. Harriet Crawford of the McDonald Institute for Archaeological Research of the University of Cambridge theorized that the Ubaid people used specialty Hadji Muhammed ceramics for festive occasions like we might bring out the fine china for special dinners today.[7]

What happened to the Ubaidians? What caused their decline? Archaeological evidence shows that Ur and Eridu were both abandoned around 3800 BCE. An eleven-foot layer of silt at Ur

---

[7] Carter & Philip, "Beyond the Ubaid," 163-168.

indicates a significant flood covered the city at that time,[8] which may also have affected nearby Eridu. The rapid, high amplitude climate change around 3700 BCE dramatically affected human settlements in this part of the world.

Global cooling resulted in glacier advancement and less snowmelt, which would have impacted the water levels of the Persian Gulf, the Tigris and Euphrates flowing from the Taurus Mountains, and Lake Hammar adjacent to Eridu. Most of the Near East, including southern Mesopotamia, experienced heightened aridity, which affected the available fresh water, made farming more complicated, and caused increases in sandstorms. These dramatic weather changes caused population shifts throughout the Near East.[9] The Ubaid people might have mostly died out from harsh conditions, with the remnants migrating to other areas and assimilating into the local populations.

---

[8] C. Leonard Woolley, "Excavations at Ur," *Journal of the Royal Society of Arts* 82, no. 4227 (1933): 46–59. http://www.jstor.org/stable/41360003.

[9] Joanne Clarke, et al. "Climatic Changes and Social Transformations in the Near East and North Africa during the 'Long' 4th Millennium BC: A Comparative Study of Environmental and Archaeological Evidence," *Quaternary*

Chapter 2: The Pre-Akkadian Period

Who were the Sumerians? What were their origins? Following the prehistoric Hassuna, Samarra, Halaf, and Ubaid cultures, the Mesopotamian powerhouse of the 4th and 3rd millennia BCE was Sumer, with cities along the Euphrates and Tigris Rivers and the Persian Gulf. The name Sumer meant "land of the civilized kings" in the Akkadian language. Some scholars believe they were an outgrowth and continuation of the Ubaid culture in Uruk. Others think they migrated into southern Mesopotamia and overcame and assimilated the remnants of the Ubaid culture.

Does linguistics give us a clue to their origins? Sumerians spoke a language isolate, which means it was unrelated to Semitic, Elamite, or any other known languages. Because the Ubaid culture was preliterate, we don't know if their language was a forerunner of the Sumerian language. Sumerian epic poetry alludes to a location north of Iran for the Sumerians' origins. Their language was agglutinative (stringing together multiple morphemes in one word), as are some languages in the Caspian Sea region.[10] However, the

---

[10] Jonathan R. Ziskind, "The Sumerian Problem

language shows complex borrowings from other languages that make it difficult to trace.[11] Whether it was a continuation of the Ubaid or migrants from the northeast, Uruk's habitation flowed uninterrupted from the Ubaid era into the Sumerian period. However, around 4000 BCE, Uruk evolved into a proper city with an elaborate culture, and an explosion of innovation began.

Several Sumerian towns grew into formidable city-states independent of other cities politically and economically. Each city had its own king who ruled the urban area and the surrounding villages and rural lands. Each city-state was like its own small country. Sometimes, one city's mighty king would take "kingship" over several other cities. According to the ancient *Sumerian King List*,[12] which dates to at least the 3rd millennium BCE, this happened cyclically—before and after the Great Flood.

The *Sumerian King List* records that after the Great Flood swept over the land, the city of Kish held "kingship" or sovereignty over other cities. Then Eanna defeated Kish and took kingship, then Uruk, then Ur, and so on. The *Sumerian King List* records that the kings before the Great Flood lived tens of thousands of years, and the kings after the flood ruled for a century or more until Gilgamesh, after which the typical reign lasted thirty years or so.

Do the long reigns represent dynasties and not individual people? Or were the pre-Gilgamesh kings simply mythical? At least some kings following Gilgamesh (and one preceding him) were real people, as inscriptions with the rulers' names and other archaeological data support their existence. But 385,200 years of eight kings before the Great Flood and 28,000 years of kings after

[11] Gonzalo Rubio, "On the Alleged 'Pre-Sumerian Substratum,'" *Journal of Cuneiform Studies* 51 (1999): 1–16. https://doi.org/10.2307/1359726.

[12] *Sumerian King List*, Translated by Jean-Vincent Scheil, Stephen Langdon, and Thorkild Jacobsen, *Livius*. https://www.livius.org/sources/content/anet/266-the-sumerian-king-list/#Translation.

the flood and before Gilgamesh and the Early Dynastic Period (circa 2900–2350 BCE) strains credibility.

The groundbreaking Sumerians surged ahead in hydraulic engineering, constructing intricate irrigation systems for crops, along with dikes and ditches to harness the perennial flooding of the Tigris and Euphrates. They were the first to build massive city walls surrounding resplendent multi-storied temples and palaces. They created imposing ziggurat towers, majestic columns, bronze decorations, and breathtaking mosaics and mural paintings with stunningly realistic figures.

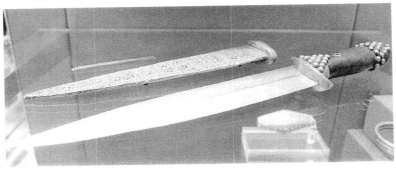

Leonard Wooley discovered this remarkable gold knife and scabbard with a lapis lazuli handle in the royal tomb of A'anepada, son of Mesannepada (circa 2550–2400 BCE).
https://commons.wikimedia.org/wiki/File:Golden_dagger_and_sheath_-_Ur_RT.jpg

Speaking of bronze, the Sumerians were probably the first—around 3300 BCE—to blend copper and tin to usher in the Bronze Age. The strength and durability of bronze produced superior weapons and tools. Astute in metallurgy, the Sumerians also worked with gold and other precious metals in the Early Bronze Age. In Ur's royal tomb, the famed archaeologist Leonard Wooley discovered the striking "dagger of Ur," with its beautifully worked, solid-gold sheath and blade and a handle grip of gold-studded lapis lazuli of the deepest blue. Other sensational finds included a golden helmet crafted with exceptional technical excellence, a golden goblet, and lyres overlaid with silver plates.[13]

The Sumerians developed the world's first writing system, initially pictographs, around 3800 BCE. Using the end of reeds, they scratched childlike symbols into wet clay that hardened, preserving their writing for millennia. These clay tablets give us astounding insight into their culture and history. The first symbols helped track sales and administrative data but not abstract concepts. Later, these symbols evolved into the more sophisticated cuneiform in which they wrote down the first literature, including epic poetry and the first law codes.

Instead of scratching pictures into the clay, they wrote cuneiform by pressing a cut reed's end into the moist clay, making stylized, wedge-shaped impressions. By 2900 BCE, they had about six hundred symbols representing words. The Sumerians opened the first schools to teach cuneiform. It took about a dozen years to memorize the symbols and gain enough proficiency to become a scribe. Other civilizations used the Sumerian cuneiform system for their own languages over the next three millennia, including the Akkadians, Elamites, Assyrians, Babylonians, and Hittites.

To the left is a cylinder seal dating to 3000 BCE or older. The recent impression of this ancient seal on damp clay is on the right. The mythical creatures depicted are serpopards—lions with serpentine necks. Flying above them are eagles with lion heads.
https://commons.wikimedia.org/wiki/File:Cylinder_seal_lions_Louvre_MNB
1167.jpg

---

[13] Woolley, "Excavations at Ur," 46–59.

In addition to writing cuneiform on wet clay, the Sumerians used elegant cylinder seals by 3500 BCE, which were similar to the stamp seals used by the Ubaid. They rolled these four-inch cylinders into damp clay, leaving an identifying picture or inscription. The cylinders were metal or semi-precious stone, like lapis lazuli or marble, and the Sumerians wore them on a lanyard around their neck or pinned to their outer robe. All social classes used cylinder seals to certify business transactions and to "sign" letters.

The Sumerians didn't invent the wheel, but they figured out how to use it for transportation. The oldest wheel found in archaeological digs was a tournette—a basic, hand-turned potter's wheel. It was found in Iran and dated to 5200 to 4700 BCE. The Sumerians developed the tournette into a freely-spinning fast potter's wheel with an axle; one dating to 3100 BCE was unearthed in Ur. Also, in Ur, Leonard Wooley uncovered a jar with a clay seal imprinted with a crude depiction of two men in a cart or chariot drawn by a donkey. This wheeled vehicle dated to about 3750 BCE. It is the earliest evidence of a wheel used for transportation![14]

The Standard of Ur—a mosaic with a lapis lazuli background and pictures of red limestone and shell that depict early four-wheeled chariots riding over bodies of dead warriors.
https://commons.wikimedia.org/wiki/File:Standard_of_Ur_chariots.jpg

---

[14] Woolley, "Excavations at Ur," 46–59.

The earliest Sumerian transportation wheels were solid disks of wood horizontally cut from a tree trunk. A hole was chiseled out in the middle of the disk, and through that, they inserted a rotating axle. The first carts quickly evolved into chariots pulled by onagers (a large horse-like donkey). Mesopotamians didn't start using horses until around 2400 BCE. These early four-wheeled chariots are pictured in the Standard of Ur mosaic, which dates to about 2600 BCE.

The Sumerians were brilliantly advanced when it came to mathematics. They started by developing a counting system using both hands, but with their method, they could go much higher than ten. On the one hand, they counted up to twelve knuckles on their four fingers. Once they got to twelve, they would hold up one finger on the other hand. Then, they'd count to twelve again and hold up the second finger. Using all four fingers and the thumb, they could count up to sixty on their two hands. The Sumerians used a sexagesimal system of counting by sixty. In our counting today, we use tens—10, 20, 30—but they would do 60, 120, 180, and so on.

By the 4th millennium BCE, the Sumerians used small clay objects to represent numbers. The number one was a tiny cone, the number ten was a little ball, and the number sixty was a larger cone. They used pictographs of these objects to write numbers as they developed writing. They ingenuously created the concept of time using a sixty-second minute and a sixty-minute hour. They divided night and day into two twelve-hour sections. By 3800 BCE, they used simple measurements, and by 2600 BCE, they were multiplying and dividing, as well as using square and cubic roots and basic geometry. By 2300 BCE, they used an abacus with the sexagesimal system.

Perhaps not as important as the wheel and writing but still an intrinsic element of Sumerian culture was beer. In the *Hymn to Ninkasi*, the goddess of beer, the Sumerians recorded the world's first known recipe for brewing beer. Sumerian beer was more like a milkshake. It was very thick and often drunk with a straw, but it had a similar alcohol content to today's beer. Instead of everyone having their own mugs, Sumerian artwork often depicts several people using long reed straws to drink from one communal jar of beer.

Aside from their beer goddess, the Sumerians worshiped a pantheon of deities with human-like images and activities. Their gods got married, had children, vied for power, cheated, robbed, and killed each other. Each city-state in Sumer—and most cultures in the rest of Mesopotamia—had a patron god or goddess. They worshiped other gods, but their patron god was the protector and champion of their city.

The primary triad of gods that ruled heaven, earth, and the underworld were An (Anu), heaven's supreme ruler; Enlil, god of the wind; and Ea (Enki), god of the earth and groundwater. Ea was the patron god of Eridu and protected humans from the Great Flood by warning a man—Utnapishtim—to build an ark to save human and animal life. Worship of these three gods pervaded most other Mesopotamian belief systems, including the Akkadians.

This cylinder seal impression pictures the god Ea (Enki).
https://commons.wikimedia.org/wiki/File:Enki(Ea).jpg

Inanna was a significant goddess throughout Mesopotamia; she was Uruk's patron deity and the goddess of beauty, love, sex, political power, and war. She later became the patron goddess of Agade, the capital of the Akkadian Empire, and she was worshiped as Ishtar by the Babylonians and Assyrians. Inanna was known for seducing human men to be her husbands, but that didn't go well for the men—one husband had to spend half the year in the underworld!

Inanna (Ishtar) was also known for repeatedly threatening to smash the gates of the underworld, getting her father (Anu) drunk, stealing the gifts of civilization for Uruk, and letting loose the Bull of Heaven because Gilgamesh spurned her marriage proposal. Ishtar figured prominently in the early life of Sargon the Great, the founder of the Akkadian Empire.

What were some key cities of Sumer, and who were their principal kings in the millennia leading up to the Akkadian Empire? Uruk and Ur were probably the second and third oldest cities. Uruk began as an Ubaid settlement around 5000 BCE and continued to exist up until the Islamic conquest around 633 CE—that is almost six thousand years! Uruk held "kingship" or dominated Sumer for about eight hundred years, beginning around 4000 BCE.

Around 3100 BCE, Uruk may have been the largest city globally with an estimated forty thousand people, plus eighty thousand more in the rural villages and smaller towns that were part of the city-state. Uruk initiated the stone construction of immense palaces and high ziggurats. In the Uruk period (4100–2900 BCE), Uruk dominated the other cities of southern Mesopotamia. It was essentially a mini-empire that served as a trade hub.

Uruk's preeminent leader in the Sumerian era was King Gilgamesh, who ruled Uruk at some point between 2800 to 2500 BCE. Although he is famous due to his myth, he was a real king. He appeared on the *Sumerian King List*, on a stone inscription in Ur, in the *Tummal Chronicle* (which says he built the Dunumunbura, Enlil's dais),[15] and on a fragment of a text found in Tell Haddad that said he was buried under the Euphrates River, which would have been temporarily diverted for his interment.

The Babylonian epic poem *Gilgamesh and Aga* has no monsters, gods, or other mythical elements; it is just an account of how Aga, King of Kish, demanded that Uruk's citizens become slaves to Kish. He wanted them to dig wells and draw water.[16] The *Sumerian King List* reports that Kish had hegemony (supremacy) over Uruk. King Gilgamesh convinced the elders to refuse Aga's

---

[15] *The Tummal Chronicle*, Livius. https://www.livius.org/sources/content/mesopotamian-chronicles-content/cm-7-tummal-chronicle/.
[16] *Gilgamesh and Aga: Translation*, The Electronic Text Corpus of Sumerian Literature, 2000. https://etcsl.orinst.ox.ac.uk/section1/tr1811.htm

orders. King Aga and his army besieged Uruk, but Gilgamesh's friend Enkidu (who is also in the *Epic of Gilgamesh*) led a successful attack. He captured Aga, and the war ended with peace between Aga and Gilgamesh.

While the *Epic of Gilgamesh* certainly contains fantastical elements, we should remember that historical events and people often acquire mythological qualities since the stories are retold and embellished over the centuries.[17] For instance, did George Washington really throw a silver dollar across the Potomac? No? Does that mean he wasn't the first president of the United States of America?

In this bas-relief, circa 2255 BCE, Gilgamesh slays the Bull of Heaven. https://en.wikipedia.org/wiki/File:O.1054_color.jpg

What is the *Epic of Gilgamesh* all about? Gilgamesh was an immoral king, deflowering the virgins of his kingdom before they could sleep with their husbands on their wedding night. His

---

[17] *The Epic of Gilgamesh*, Academy of Ancient Texts.
https://www.ancienttexts.org/library/mesopotamian/gilgamesh/.

disgruntled citizens sent a prostitute out to the wilderness to tame Enkidu, a wild man living with the beasts of the field and eating grass. After Enkidu had sex with the prostitute for days, the wild animals would have nothing more to do with him, so he agreed to go to Uruk to change the order of things.

After arriving in Uruk, Enkidu barred Gilgamesh from raping a new bride, and the two men, who were the strongest in the land, engaged in a fierce fight. Neither could overcome the other, so they kissed and became friends. Forgetting about the bride, they journeyed to Lebanon's cedar forest and killed the Humbaba monster. On their way back to Uruk, the goddess Inanna (Ishtar) fell in love with Gilgamesh, but he turned down her proposal.

Furious, Inanna demanded her father, the chief god Anu, give her the Bull of Heaven. She led it to Uruk, where it snorted and buried men in deep pits. Enkidu took the bull by the horns, and Gilgamesh killed it. However, the gods decreed that one of the men must die for killing the two divine beasts: the Humbaba monster and the Bull of Heaven. The verdict fell on Enkidu, and Gilgamesh mourned him, refusing to let him be buried until a maggot fell out of his dead friend's nose.

Confronted by his mortality, the distraught Gilgamesh then journeyed to find Utnapishtim—the Noah-like figure who built the ark to save humans and animals from the flood and became immortal. Gilgamesh failed in his quest for immortality but returned to Uruk, acknowledging his humanity and realizing the city was his destiny. Even though he would die, whatever good he would bring to Uruk would endure.

The major city of Ur was strategically situated where the Euphrates flowed into the Persian Gulf. Due to the trade from the river and the gulf, Ur was an astonishingly wealthy city. The marshland surrounding Ur provided fertile land for agriculture. A great flood ended the Ubaid settlement there around 3800 BCE, but within three centuries, the Sumerians rebuilt Ur. It grew to an estimated population of thirty-four thousand. The city of Ur was home to the Semitic forefathers of the patriarch Abraham, who probably lived near the end of the Akkadian Empire.

Ur's incredible wealth was displayed in the "death pit" discovered by Leonard Wooley in 1926. Around 2600 BCE, a great queen or priestess named Puabi was buried with over one hundred soldiers and attendants, who had been sacrificed to accompany her to the underworld. A spectacular treasure trove shared her grave. Archaeologists found a golden headdress and tableware, gold and lapis lazuli necklaces, belts, lyres, and a silver chariot.

The notable King Mesannepada of Ur overthrew Uruk's Lugal-kitun, breaking Uruk's dominance over Sumer and inaugurating Ur's First Dynasty (2500–2445 BCE). The *Sumerian King List* says he ruled for eighty years. He also ruled over the city of Kish, according to documentation in the Royal Cemetery at Ur. His son Meskiagnun was married to Queen Gan-saman, who was probably Akkadian. The bowl of Gan-Saman found in Ur had an inscription from the queen to her husband; it was written in the Akkadian language using the cuneiform script at least a century before Sargon the Great.

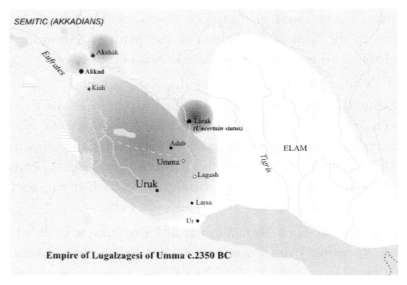

This map shows some of Mesopotamia's key cities just before the Akkadian Empire. CC BY-SA 3.0,
https://commons.wikimedia.org/w/index.php?curid=1084105

The Sumerian city of Lagash was a key artistic center on the Tigris River about fourteen miles east of Uruk. Around 2500 BCE, in its First Dynasty, Lagash was first a tributary city to Uruk and then achieved independence until the Akkadians conquered it. King Eannatum was a sensational king who built a mini-empire. He crushed the Elamite settlements on the Persian Gulf, gained ascendency over most of Sumer's cities, and pushed his territory's borders north to Akshak, encompassing the region of Akkad.

Kish was a principal city on the Euphrates in central Mesopotamia, south of Akkad's presumed location. Sargon the Great grew up as a gardener's son in Kish and served as cupbearer to King Ur-Zababa. The *Sumerian King List* said Kish was the first city to have "kingship" following the Great Flood, and it took "kingship" back several times, once by Queen Ku-Baba, a tavern keeper. The names of its earliest monarchs hint at a Semitic-Akkadian influence from its inception. Because of its location in northern Sumer, the more powerful Sumerian kings declared they were the "King of Kish" in addition to being the king of their own city; they were making the point that their kingdom extended from the south to the northern end of Sumer.

Umma on the Tigris was an unassuming city. It was never mentioned in the *Sumerian King List* as asserting kingship over the other Sumerian cities. But then, King Lugal-zage-si came to the throne, and everything changed. Lugal-zage-si began conquering one city after another: Uruk, Lagash, Ur, Nippur, Larsa, and finally Kish. He conquered Kish with the help of Sargon, who would one day become his greatest nemesis. All of Sumer fell under his control, and according to one inscription, he may have conquered as far west as the Mediterranean Sea.

Aside from Sumer, another emerging power before the Akkadian Empire was Ashur. It was located in northern Mesopotamia, and it would later rise to form the fierce Assyrian Empire after the Akkadian Empire. Semitic Akkadian-speaking pastoral herders—probably distant relations of the Akkadians—settled Ashur by 2600 BCE. The Torah said Ashur was on the Tigris River's western banks (Genesis 2:14). It was named after its founder Ashur, who was Shem's son and Noah's grandson (Genesis 10:22). Ashur grew into a city-state before the Akkadian Empire, along with other Assyrian cities, such as Nineveh, Arbela, and Gasur. The Akkadians called this region Azubinum.

The rival city-states of Sumer and the rest of Mesopotamia incessantly fought for power, goods, and territory. They formed mini-empires and took turns dominating each other. But soon, they would face the Akkadians—a power beyond their comprehension.

Chapter 3: The Rise of the Akkadian Empire

Where did he come from? Who was this man who usurped the throne of Kish, then daringly and dramatically conquered all of Mesopotamia and beyond? Wasn't Sargon just the gardener's son? How did this obscure foundling swallow up parts of modern-day Turkey, western Iran, and Syria in an age when imperialism was a novel concept? Somehow, this seemingly insignificant young man rose to incredible power and reigned from the Persian Gulf to the Mediterranean Sea. Let's explore the unprecedented rise of the Akkadian Empire and its first king, Sargon the Great, who reigned from 2334 to 2279 BCE.

A recurring theme in ancient literature is the story of an abandoned baby in a basket floating down the river—a baby who would grow up to be a revolutionary leader of a new kingdom. Romulus and his twin Remus drifted down the Tiber to be suckled by a she-wolf and then went on to found Rome. Moses floated down the Nile to be adopted by an Egyptian princess and later led the new Israelite nation. But before Romulus, Remus, and Moses, Sargon was abandoned to the river—or at least that's what an "autobiography" probably written over one thousand years after his death says.

A clay tablet dating to 1200 BCE or later supposedly reveals Sargon's birth story in his own words. We don't know whether this was a copy of an older original or if it was a fictional account. Many scholars call it a "pseudo-autobiography." We'll discuss this story more in Chapter 9, but it says Sargon's mother was a high priestess. He never knew his father, but he somehow did know that his father's family lived in the highlands in Azupiranu (an Akkadian word for "City of Saffron") on the banks of the Euphrates.

Sargon's mother conceived and gave birth to him in secret. The story doesn't say why she had to conceal the birth; presumably, she wasn't married to the father. She put him in a reed basket and set him in the river, which carried him downstream to where a man named Akki was drawing water for irrigation. Akki took him out of the water, reared him as his adopted son, and put him to work in a date grove, where the goddess Ishtar "loved" him.

Sargon and his foster father Akki lived in Kish, and they may have tended the palace garden or sold their produce to the palace. The *Sumerian King List* said that Sargon's father was a gardener, and Sargon was a cupbearer to Ur-Zababa, King of Kish. Sargon must have been an exceptional young man to rise from a humble gardener to become the king's cupbearer. A cupbearer served the king's beverages, tasting them first to ensure the wine had no poison. A cupbearer would be in the king's presence almost all of the time. He would be a trustworthy person who would see and hear all of what happened around the king. He would likely be an informal sounding board and confidante to the king.

The Sargon and Ur-Zababa tablet tells how Sargon became King Ur-Zababa's cupbearer and what happened soon after.[18] Because

---

[18] "Sargon and Ur-Zababa," *The Electronic Text Corpus of Sumerian Literature*, Oxford: Faculty of Oriental Studies, University of Oxford, 2006. https://etcsl.orinst.ox.ac.uk/cgi-bin/etcsl.cgi?text=t.2.1.4#.

the tablet was fragmented, some lines are missing, leaving one to guess what happened in some places. It begins by saying that Kish had been like a haunted town, but under its "shepherd," King Ur-Zababa, it had turned into a living settlement again. The irrigation canals flowed, the farmers' hoes tilled the land, the furnaces produced pottery and metalwork, and Kish prospered.

This mosaic from the Standard of Ur depicts a Sumerian king with his attendants.

However, the gods Enlil and An decided to terminate Ur-Zababa's reign and lift Sargon to the throne. One evening, Sargon brought the regular deliveries to the palace (presumably produce, as Sargon and his father were gardeners). The king was sleeping and had a disturbing dream but did not discuss it with anyone. However, following the vision, Ur-Zababa appointed Sargon to be his cupbearer, placing him in charge of the drinks' cupboard. His promotion resulted from the goddess Inanna's favor over Sargon.

After about a week, something happened that terrified King Ur-Zababa. Here, we have missing lines in the tablet, so what frightened him is a matter of speculation. We know that King Lugal-zage-si of Uruk, who had been systematically conquering all of Sumer's cities and leaving the Sumerians horror-stricken by his brutal ferocity, was headed his way. Or possibly Ur-Zababa may have been frightened about his health. The tablet says the king wet himself and that blood and pus were in his urine, suggesting a severe kidney infection.

At this point, Sargon had a horrific dream that the goddess Inanna drowned Ur-Zababa in a sea of blood. Sargon stirred in his sleep, groaning. When word that Sargon had a troubling dream reached the king's ears, King Ur-Zababa called Sargon to him. He asked him, "What did you dream?" Sargon told him, and Ur-Zababa bit his lip in fear. He understood the dream to mean that Sargon would assassinate him. The king believed he had to strike preemptively, so he plotted to kill Sargon before Sargon killed him!

King Ur-Zababa had Sargon deliver his bronze drinking vessels to the chief smith, Beliš-Tikal, apparently to melt them down. But the king had secretly ordered Beliš-Tikal to throw Sargon into the statue mold and cover him with the molten metal. Sargon would become a bronze statue! Fortunately, the goddess Inanna blocked Sargon's path to the temple where Beliš-Tikal worked. "This is a pure, holy temple! No one with blood on him can enter!"

Sargon apparently believed the goddess referred to his dream of blood, so he stopped at the gate. He called to the smith to come out to him on the street and handed over the drinking vessels, which the master smith took and melted them down to fill the mold. After about a week, Sargon returned to the king's palace—as a healthy man and not a statue—and Ur-Zababa shook with fear when he saw him. With his first plan foiled, Ur-Zababa conjured up a new plot.

People sent messages by writing on clay tablets in this era, but they weren't yet using envelopes for tablets. Later on, the "envelopes" were an outer layer of clay. The person receiving the letter broke the thin outer layer, revealing the message on the inner layer. Uruk's King Lugal-zage-si was marching north to conquer Kish, and King Ur-Zababa dispatched Sargon with a clay tablet message to Lugal-zage-si. The letter contained a plot to murder Sargon; lines of the story are missing here that might explain why Ur-Zababa asked his enemy to kill his cupbearer. Maybe Ur-Zababa was offering terms of surrender to Lugal-zage-si and warning him that Sargon would be a dangerous insurgent if allowed to live.

The tablet only has a few more lines, with gaps in between. Because it previously mentioned the message Sargon took to Lugal-zage-si not having an envelope, we can infer that Sargon read the letter. Ur-Zababa probably assumed that Sargon, the gardener's son, did not know how to read (and it took years to learn to read cuneiform), but perhaps Sargon had someone read the message to him. At any rate, it appears that Sargon somehow manipulated affairs to join forces with Lugal-zage-si against Ur-Zababa and Kish.

Knowing he was doomed if he continued to serve Ur-Zababa, Sargon likely switched alliances, offering his inside knowledge of palace affairs to Lugal-zage-si. Somehow, Ur-Zababa was out, and Sargon became Kish's ruler, probably as a vassal ruler under Uruk and Lugal-zage-si. When Sargon usurped Kish's throne, this may be when he took the throne name "Sargon," which came from the Akkadian word *Sarru-kin*, meaning "true king." Sargon's childhood name is unknown.

At some point, probably soon after conquering Kish, the *Sumerian King List* says Sargon built the city of Agade (Akkad). But was it already there? And if so, where? And who were the Akkadians? The Akkadians were a Semitic tribe that most likely came from the Arabian Peninsula. They migrated into central and southern Mesopotamia in the early 3rd millennium or perhaps earlier. The Semitic settlement of Agade (Akkad) may have existed as early as 2900 BCE.[19] I. J. Gelb's language studies revealed that

---

[19] D. D. Luckenbill, "Akkadian Origins," *The American Journal of Semitic Languages and Literatures* 40, no. 1 (1923): 1–13. http://www.jstor.org/stable/528139.

scribes with Akkadian names appeared on *southern* Mesopotamian tablets and inscriptions as early as 2700 BCE (almost four centuries before Sargon). Gelb believed the Akkadians had already populated northern Mesopotamia and gradually migrated south.[20] The Akkadians adopted the Sumerian cuneiform script to produce the first documented written Semitic language.

The city of Agade (Akkad) rose from obscurity to such prestige that it continued to be named in royal proclamations long after the Akkadian Empire folded. In fact, it was mentioned all the way to Cyrus the Great. Despite its renown, its ruins lie under the sands somewhere in central Mesopotamia, waiting to be discovered. Some scholars believe if Akkad was where Sargon was born—and if his mother really put him in a basket in the river—Akkad would be upstream of the Euphrates from Kish. But neither premise is certain. *The Sargon Geography* said, "from Damru to Sippar is the Land of Akkad."[21] Sippar is north of Kish, where the Euphrates and Tigris almost meet together, and from Babylonian documents, Damru appears to have been close to Kish.

Semantics scholar Christophe Wall-Romana scoured over 160 citations of Agade (Akkad) in cuneiform documents, attempting to match up geographical references to circumscribe as accurately as possible where the capital of the Akkadian Empire lay. His investigation reveals a location on or near the Tigris on the southeastern border of present-day Baghdad. He believed that since Sargon was a rival of Lugal-zage-si when he built Agade, he chose his capital in a region beyond Lugal-zage-si's scope of power.[22]

---

[20] Jerrold S. Cooper, "Sumerian and Akkadian in Sumer and Akkad," *Orientalia* 42 (1973): 239. http://www.jstor.org/stable/43079390.

[21] *The Sargon Geography*, Translated by Wayne Horowitz, *Mesopotamian Cosmic Geography*

[22] Christophe Wall-Romana, "An Areal Location of Agade," *Journal of Near Eastern Studies* 49, no. 3 (1990): 205-45. http://www.jstor.org/stable/546244.

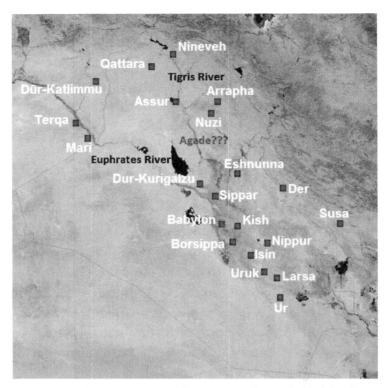

This map depicts a potential location of Agade (Akkad) on the Tigris River, between Eshnunna and Assur, southeast of present-day Baghdad. CC BY-SA 2.5,

Map modified: location of Euphrates and Tigris rivers and the possible location of Agade noted.

In the Sumerian *The Curse of Agade*, which we will discuss in Chapter 5, the city of Agade (Akkad) was a busy port city. "Its harbor, where ships docked, was filled with excitement."[23] The prologue to the Code of Hammurabi lists many Mesopotamian cities in geographical order, and it names Eshnunna, Agade, Ashur

---

[23] *The Curse of Agade*, Translated by Jerrold S. Cooper, Baltimore: Johns Hopkins University Press, 1983.

(Aššur or Assur), and Nineveh in sequence.[24] Since the other three cities all lay on the Tigris River going north from Eshnunna, perhaps Agade was on the Tigris between Eshnunna and Ashur, which fits with Wall-Romana's estimation.

The Akkadian civilization existed in northern and central Mesopotamia for hundreds of years before Sargon came to power, so it's possible Agade was already in place. Whether Sargon simply restored an older city, enlarged an existing town, or built a new city from the ground up, Agade became the capital city of Sargon's empire. The term *Akkad* also denotes the northern region of ancient Babylonia; thus, some scholars use the word *Agade* to mean the city and *Akkad* when speaking of the region.

Although Sargon and Lugal-zage-si collaborated in conquering Kish, they later became enemies. The clay tablet with the story of Sargon, Ur-Zababa, and Lugal-zage-si is severely damaged in this section, but it mentions Lugal-zage-si's wife apparently in reference to Sargon. Were they engaged in an affair or some sort of intrigue? It also says Lugal-zage-si received such dreadful news from an envoy that he cried, "Alas!" and plopped down in the dust. "Sargon does not yield!"

While Lugal-zage-si was consolidating his rule over the Sumerian cities in the south, Sargon had been amassing forces and power in northern Mesopotamia. He probably united the scattered Akkadian-speaking tribes. He was now marching with his army toward Uruk. Lugal-zage-si quickly gathered a massive army of fifty ensis. An ensi was a king of a city-state, so Lugal-zage-si called up all the princes of Sumer to fight Sargon.

In two heated battles, Sargon overwhelmed the Sumerian forces. Perhaps the Sumerian ensis weren't enthusiastic about fighting for their fierce overlord, Lugal-zage-si. Sargon besieged Uruk,

---

[24] *The Code of Hammurabi*, Translated by L.W. King, *The Avalon Project: Documents in Law, History*

demolished its walls, and captured Lugal-zage-si. He placed a yoke on Lugal-zage-si's neck and dragged him to Nippur, forcing him to walk in shame through Nippur's gate. Why Nippur? It was the god Enlil's sacred sanctuary, and Enlil was Lugal-zage-si's patron god. Sargon demonstrated that Lugal-zage-si had lost Enlil's patronage and was drained of his power.

On the pedestal of Enlil's idol, Sargon inscribed:

> "Sargon, king of Akkad, overseer of Inanna, king of Kish, anointed of Anu, king of the land, governor of Enlil. He defeated the city of Uruk and tore down its walls; in the battle of Uruk, he won, took Lugal-zage-si, king of Uruk, in the course of the battle and led him in a collar to the gate of Enlil."

The land of Sumer was now free of their cruel master, Lugal-zage-si, who had laid fire to Sumer's cities, seized their precious metals and jewels, destroyed the statues of their gods, torn down their homes, and cut off the hands of anyone who defied him. The Sumerians believed the gods had judged Lugal-zage-si for his sins.[25]

---

[25] Marvin A. Powell, "The Sin of Lugalzagesi," *Wiener Zeitschrift Für Die Kunde Des Morgenlandes* 86 (1996): 307–14. http://www.jstor.org/stable/23864744.

This copper head—possibly of Sargon—marked a shift in the artistic expression of royalty with realistic features and precise craftsmanship.

https://commons.wikimedia.org/wiki/File:Mask_of_Sargon_of_Akkad.jpg

The rise of the Akkadian Empire marked a watershed moment in Mesopotamian history—not just the empire part but also the dominance of the Semitic Akkadians over the Sumerians. From this point on, the Semitic people—the Akkadians, Assyrians, and Babylonians—held dominion for most of the rest of ancient Mesopotamia's history until the Persians invaded. Was Sargon's strife with Lugal-zage-si born out of a long-simmering racial feud, or was it simply two kings vying for power, as had happened throughout Sumer's history?

Most likely, it was simply a power encounter with no racial undertones. Neither king identified themselves as Sumerian or Semite, just king of the cities and the land. They ruled political units, not racial factions. The *Sumerian King List* reveals the royal families of Sumer switching from Sumerian to Semitic names and back again. Sumerians and Semites appeared to live peacefully together and assimilated each other's cultures. Sargon himself prayed to Sumerian gods.[26]

Sargon's bombastic royal inscriptions and other accounts contemporary with his lifetime are fragmentary; they were rewritten and probably altered by later scribes. The few materials available that date to Sargon's lifetime or shortly after are too few to form a composite picture. Many accounts of Sargon's life became available a century later, but by that time, they had degenerated into myth, leaving the task of comparing the tales with what Sargon said about himself and trying to trace what really happened. Perhaps when the city of Agade is finally discovered and resurrected from the desert sands, we can put more pieces of the puzzle together about Sargon and his successors.

---

[26] Thorkild Jacobsen, "The Assumed Conflict between Sumerians and Semites in Early Mesopotamian History," *Journal of the American Oriental Society*

Chapter 4: The Golden Age of the Akkadian Empire

In the centuries following Sargon's rule over the Akkadian Empire, the Mesopotamians—even those not Akkadian—called it their Golden Age. Although other rulers with Semitic names, like Ur-Zababa, had ruled Kish, Sargon transcended his predecessors. Sargon picked up where Lugal-zage-si left off: consolidating control of all Sumer, then expanding north into central and northern Mesopotamia. He conquered east of the great Euphrates and west of the Tigris and then extended the empire as far east as the Mediterranean and north into today's Turkey. Sargon established a military tradition and governmental style that served as a prototype for other Mesopotamian dynasties and empires. He left behind a strong legacy, which his sons and grandson held firm.

After Sargon, King of Kish and Agade, defeated Lugal-zage-si and took Uruk, he initiated successful campaigns against neighboring cities to expand his empire and acquire more resources. Since Lugal-zage-si had already consolidated all of Sumer under his rule, technically, Sargon would inherit his realm. But while the Sumerian city-states appreciated Sargon freeing them from

Lugal-zage-si, they weren't keen on coming under the yoke of another overlord—especially an upstart with no royal lineage.

Sargon was forced to lay siege to each city-state of Sumer, one after the other, beginning with Ur, Lagash, and Umma. Conquering Ur, strategically located where the Euphrates flowed into the Persian Gulf, gave Sargon power over the river traffic and the gulf. Umma was Lugal-zage-si's home city; he had ruled there for seven years before making Uruk his center of operations. Umma and Lagash had been in constant warfare with each other for centuries, as they contended over the boundary line between the two city-states until Lugal-zage-si came to power in Umma. Now, both cities fell under Sargon's dominance, which ended Lagash's First Dynasty (2500–2300 BCE).

In Sargon's victory stele, a soldier leads Sumerian prisoners. By ALFGRN https://commons.wikimedia.org/w/index.php?curid=77514888

Once Sargon gained ascendancy over all of Sumer, he turned his attention to northern Mesopotamia. For success in this endeavor, he called on a new god. Sargon had previously only mentioned the Sumerian gods in his inscriptions. He especially pointed out that Inanna had loved him as a youth and manipulated events to save him from Ur-Zababa's plots and place him on the throne. But now, he turned to the Semitic god Dagan.

Dagan is sometimes considered the Semitic version of Sumer's Enlil, the king-making god. Dagan was the father of Baal, who was worshiped in Canaan (he became a strong competitor to the Israelite god YHWH) and may be the Babylon Bel (or Marduk). Dagan was the primary Semitic god in central and northern Mesopotamia (including Agade), and the Philistines of Canaan later made him their patron god. He was the god whose head fell off when the Philistines put the stolen Israelite Ark of the Covenant in his sanctuary (Tanakh, I Samuel 5).

But that was far in the future. Sargon needed Dagan's support to conquer northern Mesopotamia and have the legitimacy to rule over the Semites. After prostrating himself before Dagan's image, Sargon tamed the Mari people east of the Euphrates and their rivals, the Ebla, to the south of Aleppo in Syria. Sargon gave Dagan credit for bestowing him the upper lands of the Euphrates, which probably included part of Anatolia (Turkey).

The "King of Battle" is an epic Akkadian story of how Akkadian merchants in Purushanda (present-day Turkey) were disputing the despotic ruler of the region, Nur-Dagan.[27] After asking Sargon to intervene, he attacked Nur-Dagan before he knew what was happening and brought that region under Akkadian control, making lucrative trade with Turkey all the easier. Sargon then headed east, raiding Canaan (Israel), Lebanon, and Syria four times. The "King

---

[27] Joan Goodnick Westenholz, *Legends of the Kings of Akkade: The Texts*, Winona Lake: Eisenbrauns, 1997.

of Battle" records that he sailed into the Mediterranean to "Kuppara," which is likely Cyprus or Crete.

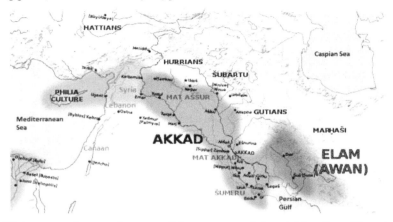

This map shows the possible extent of the Akkadian Empire under Sargon.

Map modified: zoomed-in, labels of seas and regions added.
https://commons.wikimedia.org/wiki/File:Moyen_Orient_3mil_aC.svg

Sargon invaded Elam's deserts and the Zagros Mountains (in modern-day Iran) and conquered the Elamite capital of Susa in the lower Zagros Mountains. To celebrate his outstanding victory in Elam, Sargon erected a massive diorite victory stele, picturing himself and his military forces. He conquered the Awan north of Susa and asserted control over the Marhashi (possibly in the Kerman region of south-central Iran), gaining access to trade in alabaster vases and valuable stones.

In *The Legend of Sargon*—his supposed autobiography discovered in the ruins of Nineveh's Library of Ashurbanipal—Sargon recounts a rebellion while he was in his "old age."

> "In my old age of 55, all the lands revolted against me, and they besieged me in Agade [Akkad], but the old lion still had teeth and claws, I went forth to battle and defeated them: I knocked them over and destroyed their vast army. Now, any king who wants to call himself my equal, wherever I went, let him go!"

The "Reign of Sargon" details how the "old lion" fought back against the rebels.[28]

"Afterward, in his old age, all the lands revolted against him, and they besieged him in Akkad; and Sargon went forth to battle and defeated them; he accomplished their overthrow and their wide-spreading host he destroyed.

Afterward, he attacked the land of Subartu in his might, and they submitted to his arms, and Sargon settled that revolt and defeated them; he accomplished their overthrow, and their wide-spreading host he destroyed, and he brought their possessions into Akkad. The soil from the trenches of Babylon he removed, and the boundaries of Akkad he made like those of Babylon."

Sargon and his wife, Queen Tashlultum, had at least four sons: Manishtushu, Rimush, Shu-Enlil, and Ilaba'is-takal. Sargon reigned for a total of fifty-five years. Rimush succeeded Sargon at his death, and Manishtushu succeeded Rimush. Sargon's daughter, the priestess Enheduanna, was a poetess and hymn writer. One famous hymn was the "Exaltation of Inanna," which was sung in the worship of the goddess for hundreds of years.

How well did Sargon's descendants perpetuate his legacy? Were they successful in continuing the remarkable expansion of the Akkadian Empire? Curiously, Rimush ascended the throne in 2279 BCE upon his father's death, although Manishtushu was his older brother, according to the *Sumerian King List*. Some scholars venture that Sargon passed over Manishtushu because rebellions kept cropping up, which Rimush's more ruthless nature could better manage. Rimush immediately faced a Sumerian insurrection. For five decades, they had simmered with resentment under

---

[28] "The Reign of Sargon," George W. Botsforth, ed., *A Source-Book of Ancient History*, New York: Macmillan, 1912. 27-28.
http://www.thelatinlibrary.com/imperialism/readings/sargontablet.html

Sargon's rule. Perhaps they could overcome the son with the "strong man" dead.

In Rimush's early years as king, six city-states revolted: Adab, Der, Kassala, Lagash, Umma, and Ur. Rimush brutally quelled the subversive cities. He bragged of obliterating massive populations, flattening cities, and even uprooting their substructures. In a series of three vicious wars in Sumer, he sent shockwaves through the land with the mass slaughter of 110,000 men, which was most of the adult male population of the six rebel cities.

He exiled another twenty-five thousand people and enslaved twenty-nine thousand, sending them to cut stone in Elam's mines. The conquered cities stood virtually empty, so he confiscated 134,000 hectares of ancestral farmland around Umma and Lagash, parceling them out to the new Akkadian landholding elite. The desolate survivors of Umma and Lagash could only remember the years they'd spent in strife over the boundary line between them; now, the land was lost to strangers.

Babylon also rebelled, and Rimush struck the city with the same merciless violence that extinguished the Sumerian insurrection. He was equally harsh against the Akkadians—his own people. One example was Kassala, which was located near Kish on the Euphrates. Kassala had resisted Sargon and reaped his vengeance. "Against Kassala he marched, and he turned Kassala into mounds and heaps of ruins; he destroyed the land and left not enough for a bird to rest thereon."[29]

The people of Kassala rebuilt their flattened city and then had the audacity to revolt against Rimush. Repeating his father's harsh reaction, he massacred twelve thousand Akkadian rebels, enslaved five thousand, and turned Kassala back into a "heaps of ruins."

---

[29] "The Reign of Sargon," Botsforth, ed., pp. 27-28.

Once Rimush regained his father's territories in Mesopotamia, he launched military campaigns in Elam, consolidating his father's conquests there. While he had been busy slaughtering Sumerians, the Elamites had formed a coalition under the Marhashi king to resist further expansion into their territories. Rimush successfully subdued the alliance and took Elam and its capital Susa back under Akkadian hegemony.

Although Rimush did not extend his father's empire, he recouped some areas that had attempted to regain independence. He ended his nine-year reign with approximately the same borders as in his father's day, but Akkad was much more prosperous. Rimush had brought back astonishing riches from Elam. At Enlil's sanctuary in Nippur, he dedicated massive amounts of copper and gold. He erected a statue of himself in tin, which was a rare metal in those days. His inscription on his sculpture, which stood before Enlil's image, said he counted himself among the gods.[30]

Rimush stopped commissioning pompous inscriptions and images of himself in the year or two before he died. What happened? Did he simply take it easy after regaining his father's territory? Was he sick or depressed? Was he dealing with internal conflict? The latter may have been true, as his own statesmen bludgeoned him to death with their cylinder seals. Since the seals were only three to five inches of metal or marble hanging on a lanyard, it would have been a long, merciless death for a man who showed no pity to his rivals.

[30] Benjamin R. Foster, *The Age of Agade: Inventing Empire in Ancient Mesopotamia*, (New York: Routledge, 2016), 6-8.

This copper alloy head is probably an Akkadian king, but his identity is unknown.

https://commons.wikimedia.org/wiki/File:Head_of_a_ruler_ca_2300_2000_BC_Iran_or_Mesopotamia_Metropolitan_Museum_of_Art_(dark_background).jpg

Why was he assassinated? If he had fallen into a state of lethargy or suffered mental or physical illness, his courtiers might have felt the empire needed a healthy, active ruler. Then, there were his atrocities. Killing off most of the male population in key Sumerian and Akkadian cities was terrible for the empire. If cities were flattened, they were not producing food and other goods necessary for the entire empire's survival.

With key civilized settlements along the Persian Gulf or the Euphrates or Tigris Rivers decimated, bandits and pirates could disrupt trade caravans and ships bringing goods to Agade. The demoralizing effect would have been horrific, especially with the cities closer to Agade like Kassala and Babylon. For all we know, some of his assassins could have been from Kassala or Babylon seeking revenge.

After Rimush was beaten to a pulp, his older brother Manishtushu succeeded him in 2279 BCE. He ruled for fourteen years. Manishtushu was an ambitious, energetic king who expanded the empire through diplomacy and military conquests, and he implemented significant internal changes. Considering his brother's assassination, Manishtushu was adamant about forming a new administrative council of men he could trust. So, he devised a land plan, building on his brother's earlier land reallocation.

He bought the ancestral farmlands of 964 men in the region of Akkad. They probably had little choice in the matter; the price they received was worth only what the farms would have produced in two years. But the fields bordered the royal lands, and Manishtushu planned to allocate this property to reward those who had served him faithfully, such as his administrators, military leaders, scribes, and priests. His devoted servants came from all points of the empire, not just Agade. He desired to establish a new Akkadian elite with undivided loyalty to him.[31]

---

[31] Foster, *The Age of Agade*, 1.

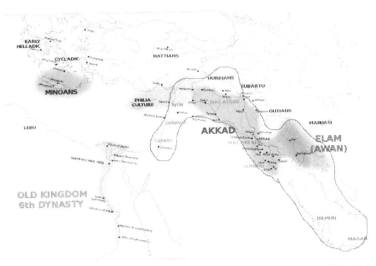

This map depicts the possible extension of the Akkadian Empire during Manishtushu's reign from where it was at the end of his father Sargon's reign.

Map modified: zoomed-in, names of regions added, outline of expanded territory inserted.
https://commons.wikimedia.org/wiki/File:Ancient_Near_East_2300BC.svg

Manishtushu benefited from his brother's ironfisted subjugation of rebellions within the empire. With relative peace established, Manishtushu could launch new expansion campaigns to strategic regions for trade. His first expansion involved subjugating or making shrewd alliances with thirty-two kings to control the entire Persian Gulf. He sailed from port to port, negotiating with friendly kings and conquering any who resisted, keeping the Persian Gulf waters free of invaders and pirates. Manishtushu then invaded Elam—for the third time since his father's reign—this time from the Persian Gulf. He plundered Susa's silver mines and set up Akkadian governors in key Elamite cities. He negotiated trade with thirty-seven other states up the Tigris River to its headwaters in eastern Turkey's Taurus Mountains.

As he expanded his empire, Manishtushu erected duplicate images of himself throughout his territories, with each inscription honoring the patron deity of the specific city. He was particularly proud of his Persian Gulf expedition and never missed the chance to mention it in his inscriptions. Manishtushu was a diplomatic master in recognizing his conquered city-states' gods and celebrating his foreign expansion, which brought astounding wealth to Mesopotamia. This was in stark contrast to the boastings of his father and brother of their cruel suppression of local rebellions.

Despite his diplomatic skills and military successes, Manishtushu met his brother's fate, as he was assassinated by his own officials. Naram-Sin, Manishtushu's son and Sargon's grandson, was crowned the Akkadian Empire's fourth king, and he who would elevate the empire to its grandest power. He followed in the footsteps of his father and grandfather, with triumphant conquests of the Lullubi people in the Elamite-Zagros Mountain region. He signed a treaty and married Elamite King Khita's daughter.

Naram-Sin's most significant test came early in his reign when he faced the Great Revolt of eighteen key Sumerian cities. This was led by King Iphur-Kish of Kish, and it included Uruk, Adab, Cutha, Isin, Kish, Lagash, Nippur, Sippar, Umma, and Ur. The Sumerians even joined forces with the Amorite nomads, who they usually considered a dire threat. Iphur-Kish directly attacked Agade, but Naram-Sin marshaled his forces and marched out to defend Agade. With the first battle won, he chased the remnants of the rebels to Kish, filling the Euphrates with dead bodies.

King Amar-girid of Uruk rallied the rest of the Sumerian coalition. He invited the Assyrians to the north to join in, but they held back. Naram-Sin attacked the Amorites first, then met Amar-girid's massive force and defeated them, capturing Amar-girid. Following this victory, Naram-Sin cut a swathe through Sumer and went down and around the Persian Gulf, pillaging and amassing great spoils of war. After winning nine battles in one year against the Mesopotamians, the people of Agade asked him to be their patron god of their city, making him equal to Inanna, Enlil, Enki, and the rest of the pantheon. He permitted them to build his temple in Agade, which many believed to be his downfall.

Naram-Sin continued with his brilliant military campaigns in Oman, Ebla (northern Syria), the Taurus Mountains, the Amanus (Nur) Mountains of south-central Turkey, and the Ararat region of Armenia. He followed the Tigris River north into the Taurus Mountains, tracing it to Hazer Lake, a rift lake 3,773 feet above sea level. He likewise followed the Euphrates up to the Karasu River, then to its source at Mount Dumlu.

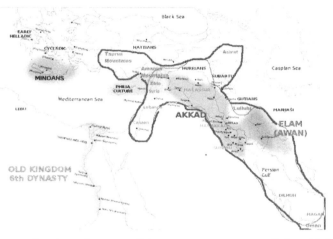

This map depicts the possible greatest extent of the Akkadian Empire under Naram-Sin. It may have considerably shrunk before he died.

Map modified: zoomed-in, regions and seas added, an outline of expanded territory inserted.
https://commons.wikimedia.org/wiki/File:Ancient_Near_East_2300BC.svg

Naram-Sin proudly called himself the "Ruler of the Four Corners of the Universe," but trouble loomed ahead. *The Curse of Agade*, which was written centuries later, said that Naram-Sin somehow incurred the wrath of the god Enlil, who retaliated by bringing famine, plague, and an invasion of the Gutian tribes to the east. Although Naram-Sin expanded the Akkadian Empire to its greatest extent, he may have lost significant portions before his death in 2217 BCE.

Sargon's conquest of all of Sumer and then all of Mesopotamia joined the Akkadians and Sumerians under one language and one government. The Akkadian Empire stretched thousands of miles at its zenith, encompassing multiple ethnic groups from the Persian Gulf to as far north as Ararat and west to the Mediterranean. He established a vision for future conquerors of what could be achieved in one lifetime. No one before him had conquered such a vast territory. He was truly the world's first emperor.

Chapter 5: The Decline and Fall of the Akkadian Empire

Naram-Sin's reign was the beginning of the end for the Akkadian Empire. Soon, it would slide into decline and ultimately crumble into oblivion. The end didn't seem near, not when Naram-Sin was winning one brilliant conquest after another. But then something happened that turned the tide, eventually closing the chapter on the Akkadian Empire after only 180 years of existence. The Mesopotamians believed Naram-Sin brought down a curse on Agade and all of Mesopotamia.

The Curse of Agade is a quasi-historical story written during Ur's Third Dynasty (2047–1750 BCE), but it is probably based on older stories. It's an example of Mesopotamian Naru literature, which portrays a king or other hero in a moralistic tale of human relationships with the divine. The *Epic of Gilgamesh* and *The Legend of Sargon* are two other examples of Naru literature.

The Curse of Agade tells how Naram-Sin offended the god Enlil and brought down devastation on all of Mesopotamia. What did Naram-Sin do to offend Enlil? The story does not divulge this information, but it could have been that he received his people's adulation as the god of Agade. It all began when several points of his extensive empire rose simultaneously in rebellion. An inscription at the base of a statue recorded Naram-Sin's victory:

"Naram-Sin the mighty, king of Agade, when the four quarters of the earth attacked him together, through the love of Ishtar bore him was victorious in nine battles in a single year and captured the kings whom they had raised against him."

This carving shows Naram-Sin at the top of his victory stele, standing on the bodies of conquered Lullubi warriors.

https://commons.wikimedia.org/wiki/File:Naram-Sin.jpg

Following this splendid triumph, Naram-Sin called himself the "mighty god of Agade" in an inscription, essentially claiming to be the city's patron god. However, the goddess Inanna, Sargon's patroness, had established her sanctuary in Agade, at least according to *The Curse of Agade*. It said Inanna spent sleepless nights ensuring Agade's people had plenty to eat, good things to drink, and rejoiced together at holidays. Inanna was the city's patroness, but Naram-Sin overturned the divine order.

The Curse of Agade said Inanna even brought monkeys, elephants, and other exotic animals to amuse the citizens in the public square.[32] Inanna brought gold, silver, copper, tin, and lapis lazuli into the city, filling the granaries with precious metals and stones. She gave the old women the gift of wise counsel, the old men the gift of eloquence, the young women the gift of entertaining, the young men the gift of military might, and the children the gift of joy.

But after caring for Agade so tenderly, Inanna received disquieting news. The story doesn't say what the unsettling news was; perhaps it was some dreadful sin of the city or its king Naram-Sin. The god Enlil reduced Agade to trembling and even terrified Inanna, who abandoned her sanctuary and left Agade, carrying with her the gift of battle and handing it over to Agade's enemy. One by one, the other gods took back the blessings they had bestowed on Agade. Ninurta took back the royal crown and throne of kingship, Utu took back the city's eloquence, Enki took back its wisdom and tore away its mooring pole, and An (Anu) took away the fear the city held over others.

One night, King Naram-Sin had a vision that the god Enlil would no longer permit Agade to be a pleasant, enduring city; instead, its temples would shake, and its treasures would be scattered. The king

---

[32] *The Curse of Agade*, Trans. Jerrold S. Cooper, (Baltimore: Johns Hopkins University Press, 1983). https://etcsl.orinst.ox.ac.uk/section2/tr215.html.

didn't tell anyone about his dream, but he donned mourning garments and gave away his royal paraphernalia. He mourned for seven years! "Who has ever seen a king burying his head in his hands for seven years?" He performed divination on the entrails of a baby goat, trying to discover the source of Enlil's displeasure, but he received no omen, even after two tries.

Exasperated with the god Enlil, Naram-Sin mobilized his troops, marched to the holy city of Nippur, and demolished Enlil's temple. He hewed it down with axes and dug up its foundation with spades. He piled up all the temple's wood and lit a huge bonfire, and he plundered the temple's gold, silver, copper, and precious gemstones. As he pilfered and destroyed Enlil's temple, good sense and intelligence left Agade.

Archaeologists unearthed the Nippur Temple in 1893. Naram-Sin's son Shar-Kali-Sharri rebuilt the temple, and Ur-Nammu of Ur's Third Dynasty and other kings renovated it.

Now, the god Enlil was like a roaring typhoon that decimated the entire land, like a tidal wave that crushes everything before it. He gazed at the eastern mountains and called out the Gutians, "an unbridled people, with human intelligence but canine instincts and monkeys' features." The Gutians swept down into Akkad like great flocks of birds. "Nothing escaped their clutches." They drove the herds of goats and cows out of their pens and dislodged the city gates of Agade.

The region became like prehistoric times before cities were established. The fields were untended, no fish were in the neglected canals, and the orchards did not yield fruit without irrigation. The rains stopped, and no plants grew. "People were flailing themselves from hunger." They were starving and dying in their homes with no one to bury them. Roving dogs would attack and kill anyone in the street.

For seven days and nights, the cities' old men and old women raised a lament to Enlil. The other gods—the patrons of the other cities ravaged along with Agade—prayed to Enlil, cooling his heart like water. They cursed Agade and asked Enlil to pour out his wrath on that city and spare the others. And so, despite the earlier devastation of all Mesopotamia, the Akkadian Empire fell completely. This was not something that happened suddenly, but the troubles that would bring its ultimate destruction began. Within three decades, the empire would shrivel, but the Sumerian cities— Ur in particular—would rise to glory once again.

We have no other historical accounts that Naram-Sin ever attacked Nippur and destroyed its temple to Enlil. However, the recorded "Year Names" of his son Shar-Kali-Sharri report that between the fourth and tenth years of his reign, he appointed a general to oversee the building of the temple of Enlil in Nippur. He laid the foundations and cut down cedar timbers to build the temple. A temple had already been in Nippur for centuries, but this was a complete rebuilding from the foundations up. As recounted in the story, the Gutians did invade, the rains really stopped, and vast numbers of people died or were displaced throughout Mesopotamia.

The brunt of the double curse of drought and invasion fell on Naram-Sin's son, Shar-Kali-Sharri, who ascended the throne upon his father's death in 2217. He ruled for twenty-four years. He was an exemplary military strategist but was stymied by a horrific drought that led to the loss of three-quarters of the northern Mesopotamian settlements. He struggled against vicious raids by the Gutian tribes to the east until he captured their king, Sharlag. High taxes on tributary states led to rebellions, but he successfully fended off Amorite invasions.

What was this massive drought that caused a severe decline in agricultural production and weakened the empire? One of human history's most devastating climate changes—the 4.2-kiloyear BP aridification event—struck the earth around 2200 to 2000 BCE, with colder temperatures and a 30 to 50 percent reduction in rainfall in Mesopotamia, Syria, and Turkey.[33] Although the extreme drought ended in about two centuries, research on Iran's lakes and the Dead Sea demonstrates that the Middle Eastern rainfall never returned to the amounts before the drought.

Changing wind and ocean currents led to erratic weather patterns. This caused the ghastly drought, and there was also a terrible series of volcanic eruptions to the north in modern-day Turkey. Archaeological evidence and soil analysis show that the sudden climate change induced calamitous degradation of arable land. Cities and entire regions were left abandoned, leading to the collapse of the Akkadian Empire.

Leilan was a small city of twenty thousand inhabitants on the border of Syria and Iraq in the Akkadian Empire's breadbasket. Archaeological and geological investigations indicate that Leilan and two nearby cities were suddenly and completely evacuated, and a fourth city lost 80 percent of its population. Naram-Sin's fortress at Tell Brak was abandoned, with unfinished walls and floors. In Leilan, the Akkadian administrative building that had been storing,

---

[33] Harvey Weiss, *Megadrought and Collapse*. New York: Oxford University Press, 2017, 94-183.

processing, and redistributing grain for a century was abruptly deserted.[34]

Nagar (Tell Brak) in northern Mesopotamia, including Naram-Sin's fortress, was abruptly deserted in the middle of a construction project around 2200 BCE.
https://commons.wikimedia.org/wiki/File:TellBrakTW-W.jpg

Archaeologists found a half-inch layer of volcanic ash on Tell Leilan dating to 2200 BCE, which likely came from the fallout of volcanic eruptions in Turkey. Volcanic ash and gasses can remain suspended in the atmosphere for years, blocking the sun and cooling temperatures. However, that alone could not account for the widespread drought throughout the Middle East (and beyond) that lasted for at least two centuries. Even before the volcanoes, soil analysis showed a marked contrast in sand and dust deposits, pointing to higher aridity and dust storms, while earlier eras had rich, moist soil.

Drought and global cooling not only devastated the Akkadian Empire but also affected all of the Middle East. It may have collapsed Egypt's Old Kingdom and perhaps even the Liangzhu

---

[34] Weiss, *Megadrought and Collapse*, 94-183.

culture of China and the Indus Valley civilization, although not all scientists are convinced it was a global event. Some scientists also argue that Mesopotamia experienced an enormous population growth—probably due to the relative peace and enhanced wealth brought by the Akkadian Empire—which was unsustainable in the semi-arid land even without climate change.[35]

While the empire was still expanding, vast regions in northern Mesopotamia suddenly emptied around 2200 BCE. Where did they go? The surviving populations of these cities were apparently part of a southern migration to Sumer. Why south? Didn't Sumer get hit by the drought as well? Yes, it did, but Sumer could manage deficits in rainfall.

Before the drought, northern Mesopotamia had more rainfall than southern Mesopotamia (it still does) and relied chiefly on rain for their crops. They had not developed the Sumerians' advanced irrigation system that had been used in central and southern Mesopotamia for two millennia. Sumer never relied much on rainfall for their crops. Although the Tigris and Euphrates suffered a 30 to 50 percent reduction in water flow, the Sumerians reconstructed their canal systems to adjust for the change. They continued as usual with their agricultural endeavors.

The drying up of grasslands in northern Mesopotamia and Syria displaced Amorite herders. They migrated south to the regions along the Euphrates delta, where the grass still grew. This led to the construction of a 110-mile "Amorite repelling" wall in Sumer. The Amorites never left central Mesopotamia and later formed the Babylonian Empire. This massive population shift of northern Mesopotamian agriculturalists and nomadic herders led to the

[35] D. Lawrence, A. Palmisano, and M. W. de Gruchy, "Collapse and Continuity: A Multi-proxy Reconstruction of Settlement Organization and Population Trajectories in the Northern Fertile Crescent during the 4.2kya Rapid Climate Change Event," *PLoS One.* 16 (1) (2021). https://pubmed.ncbi.nlm.nih.gov/33428648/.

Akkadian Empire's fall, the doubling of Sumer's population, and the rise of Ur's Third Dynasty.[36]

What about the other part of the curse, the Gutian invasion? Who were the Gutians, the "fanged snake of the mountain ranges?" They were of mysterious origins and non-literate; thus, tracing these people linguistically is challenging. We only have the names of some of their kings recorded in Akkadian and Sumerian documents. They lived east of the Tigris River in the Zagros Mountains of present-day Iran, and they paid tribute to Sumerian King Lugal-Anne-Mundu of Adab before the Akkadian Empire era.

They were also under Sargon the Great's overlordship, but when his grandson Naram-Sin came to the throne, they were no longer docilely paying tribute. On one of his victory steles, Naram-Sin recorded a battle in which the Gutians killed one-quarter of his 360,000-man army before he finally conquered their king, Gula'an. The *Weidner Chronicle*—a Babylonian history written around 1800 BCE—said the god Marduk, Babylon's patron god, summoned the Gutians against Naram-Sin because he had attacked and demolished Babylon.[37] But the Gutians were unschooled in showing reverence to the gods and offended Marduk, so he removed them from the land.

The Gutians had been slowly filtering into Mesopotamia during Naram-Sin's reign. After his death, his son, King Shar-Kali-Sharri, fought bitterly against the Gutian hordes that suddenly increased right about when Mesopotamia fell into its two-hundred-year dry spell. The Gutians were notorious for raiding parties. They launched guerrilla attacks, devastated cities, and stripped the fields of their produce. Shar-Kali-Sharri finally captured their king,

---

[36] Weiss, *Megadrought and Collapse*, 94-183.

[37] *Weidner Chronicle (ABC 19)*, Livius, 2020. https://www.livius.org/sources/content/mesopotamian-chronicles-content/abc-19-weidner-chronicle/.

Sharlag, in the year after he finished building Enlil's temple in Nippur, which subdued the Gutians for a time.

This vase fragment depicts a prisoner of the Akkadians being pulled by a nose ring and with a distinctive braid. He may have been Gutian.

https://commons.wikimedia.org/wiki/File:Prisoner_of_the_Akkadian_Empire_period_possibly_Warka_ancient_Uruk_LOUVRE_AO_5683.jpg

Shar-Kali-Sharri spent the next three years victoriously fighting the nomadic Amorites who had suddenly migrated into the Euphrates River region because of the drought. For two years after that, Shar-Kali-Sharri took the battle against the Gutians to their territory, fighting in Elam and bringing them "under the yoke" in his seventeenth year as king. Shar-Kali-Sharri died in 2193 BCE as the last king of the Akkadian Empire. The *Sumerian King List* summarized the anarchy following his death when four usurpers vied for power as the empire dwindled: "Then who was king? Who was not the king? Igigi, Imi, Nanum, Ilulu: four of them ruled for only three years."

The Sumerian cities, one by one, declared their independence from Akkad. They had the upper hand now. Agade was no longer the seat of a fearsome overlord. The drought wasn't affecting Sumer as much as in the north—they weren't starving and dying with no one to bury them. The region of Akkad was experiencing a precipitous drop in its population, while Sumer was growing, as it was able to sustain the people through irrigation.

During this period of instability, the marauding Gutian tribes swept back down from the mountains into Akkad and Sumer. This time, the Akkadians could not defend themselves from the catastrophic raids; the Gutian strikes on river traffic and camel caravans destroyed the trade routes. The drought had already caused lethal food shortages, and now, the Gutians stripped anything that was still growing, plunging Akkad into a gruesome famine.

The Gutians weren't the only invaders. The Elamites, Hurrians, and Lullubi formed an eastern coalition of sixteen hostile kings, taking advantage of Agade's weakness. Although initially repulsed, they attacked again, dealing the Akkadians a crushing blow. The *Cuthean Legend of Naram-Sin* also mentions the mysterious Umman-Manda people as another adversary. They possibly came from central Turkey.

Finally, in 2189 BCE, Dudu grasped Akkad's crown—but the empire was no more. It had crumbled away, leaving only Agade, Kish, and Eshnunna. Was Dudu part of the Sargonic dynasty or just another usurper? The *Sumerian King List* doesn't say who he was, only that he ruled twenty-one years. The only records available say that King Dudu campaigned against Umma and Lagash, bringing home spoils of war.

Dudu's son Shu-turul came to the throne in 2168 BCE. He was the last king of the three cities and ruled for fifteen years. After this, Akkad and much of Mesopotamia fell into the "Dark Ages" under the power of the fierce Gutians. The Gutian nomads seemed disinterested in farming except for small garden plots inside the cities. They let the sheep, goats, and cattle out of their pens to roam the land. The famine deepened in the regions they controlled, and trade came to a standstill. The canals filled with sediment, and grass covered the highways.

Meanwhile, around 2091 BCE, the "Sumerian Renaissance" arose with the Third Dynasty of Ur. Power shifted to the south as the people fled famine and invasion, emptying northern Mesopotamia. Ur would not be an empire like Akkad, but it controlled southern Mesopotamia for the next century. It restored the Sumerian language, although Akkadian continued to be used in trade and diplomacy for the next thousand years.

Climate change and invasions obliterated the Akkadian civilization, yet the empire had joined multiple cultures in its immense melting pot, sharing a common language. They showed the world what an empire looked like and set the benchmark for future empires. That legacy would endure.

Chapter 6: Akkadian Society and Daily Life

Akkad itself and all its conquered lands represented real people. What did daily life look like in the Akkadian Empire? What did the people eat and drink, what did they wear, what were their houses like, and what was their marital and social structure? This chapter will examine the literature and artifacts of the Akkadian Empire era, opening a window to the past on how people lived their lives.

The Akkadian Empire encompassed numerous nationalities and cultures. Could the conquered people preserve their cultures? Although the empire was one political unit, the conquered regions outside Mesopotamia continued with their ethnic and social traditions. Most areas within Mesopotamia continued to follow the Sumerian culture, which the Akkadians assimilated, including praying to a similar pantheon of gods. When we use the word "Akkadian" for people, it doesn't necessarily mean the Semitic ethnicity of the original Akkadian speakers. We can't even be sure if Sargon was ethnically Akkadian since his birth parents are unknown. In a broad sense, the term for Akkadian people means those from varying backgrounds who embraced the Akkadian king's worldview and culture.[38]

Speaking of Akkadian and Sumerian, did the Sumerians have to learn the Akkadian language? What language did the empire use for literature, administration, and governmental affairs? For centuries, the Sumerians and the Semitic Akkadians lived together in central and southern Mesopotamia. When the Akkadian Empire rose to power, most Mesopotamians were already bilingual in Sumerian and Akkadian. The two languages, although they were entirely different, borrowed from each other freely up to and through the Akkadian Empire until they became a *sprachbund*—a linguistic crossroads. The Akkadian language replaced spoken Sumerian by the end of the empire.

However, southern Mesopotamians still used Sumerian in religious ceremonies and literature for the next two thousand years, similar to Latin in more recent times. The Akkadians adopted the Sumerian cuneiform script, so their administrative and governmental affairs used spoken and written Akkadian. Following the collapse of the Akkadian Empire, the Akkadian language divided into two Semitic dialects: Assyrian (used in northern Mesopotamia) and Babylonian (used in central and southern Mesopotamia).

What about outside of Mesopotamia? The Akkadian language was similar to the Semitic languages spoken in the easternmost parts of the empire—Syria, Lebanon, and Canaan. Thus, the conquered Semitic people could quickly pick up the spoken Akkadian language. Learning the cuneiform script would have been much more difficult. The Semitic languages outside Mesopotamia were most likely preliterate, as the Proto-Sinaitic script (the earliest alphabet) did not emerge until about 1900 BCE.

---

[38] Foster, *The Age of Agade*, 30-33.

When the British and French first began archaeological digs in Mesopotamia in the 1800s, they unearthed twenty-four thousand tablets in the Akkadian region of Nineveh. They discovered so many bas-reliefs (sculptures that project out slightly from a stone slab) that they would stretch almost two miles if stood side by side. These fascinating bas-reliefs recorded the great kings' wars and achievements. But to understand what these tablets and reliefs said, the archaeologists had to decipher the cuneiform script, which hadn't been done yet.[39]

So, the linguistic experts set to work, and it took them about ten years to decipher the texts. The cuneiform script contains approximately six hundred characters. Some of these represented whole words (like with Chinese, Korean, or Japanese today), while others represented syllables. Each character or sign could represent both a syllable and a word or even multiple words. It all depended on context.

Because each written cuneiform symbol could represent multiple values, some detractors believed it could never be translated. They scoffed at the accuracy of the early translations. To address this question, the Royal Asiatic Society sent copies of a newly discovered inscription to four well-known linguists in 1856. Each linguist had to translate the inscription without consulting any of the others. Six weeks later, the committee examined the four translations, and they were remarkably uniform![40]

The Akkadians and other Mesopotamians kept meticulous records using cuneiform script, covering the minutiae of daily life, such as sales, property information, business transactions, and even their histories. They didn't have numbered years in the Akkadian era, so they remembered dates by the years' names or a ruler's year

---

[39] Karen Rhea Nemet-Nejat, *Daily Life in Ancient Mesopotamia*, (Westport, Connecticut: Greenwood Press, 1998), 4.

[40] Nemet-Nejat, *Daily Life*, 4-5.

in office. For instance, an inscription might read, "In Naram-Sin's fifth year," and notable events described different years of a king's rule, like "the year the temple's foundation was laid" or "the year Elam was put under the yoke."

A surprisingly abundant source of cuneiform family archives and letters gives us a glimpse of what family life and women's roles were like in the Akkadian Empire. Young men usually married in their twenties, but their brides were in their teens; they could have been as young as fourteen. Fathers might arrange a marriage for their daughters when they were still little girls. Thus, a girl of six or seven could be called a "wife" in an *inchoate* marriage once her father received the bride price.[41]

An inchoate marriage meant that a couple gradually entered into the marriage in stages rather than in a single ceremony. A girl lived at home with her parents after the betrothal in the prenuptial stage, which could extend for a decade. If any other man attempted to have sexual relations with her, he could receive the death penalty as a rapist of a married woman. The Akkadian word *batultu* meant virgin, and a woman was expected to be a virgin until she began living with her husband, although kissing and intimate touching seemed to be allowed.

When the young woman began living with her husband in the connubial stage, she brought a dowry. Her husband could not do anything with that money or property—they were for the woman and her future children. If she died without children, the dowry returned to her family, and the husband got his bride price back. Once a woman had a child with her husband, the marriage was complete, meaning it was no longer inchoate. If she died with children, the money was her children's inheritance; it would not go back to her birth family.

---

[41] M. Stol, "Women in Mesopotamia," *Journal of the Economic and Social History of the Orient* 38, no. 2 (1995): 125. http://www.jstor.org/stable/3632512.

Most marriage contracts were oral, not written. Written contracts were used if the bride or groom owned considerable property or a substantial bride price or dowry was at stake. However, the bride's father and the bridegroom could negotiate issues like whether the groom could take a second wife or concubine if the wife couldn't conceive. What would be the bride's status in the home if a second wife or concubine entered the picture?[42]

Most marriages were a husband with one wife unless the wife could not conceive or had a chronic illness. Then the husband usually took a second wife, but the first wife could sometimes choose the second wife or concubine. The biblical Abraham lived in Ur, Harran (Turkey), and Canaan toward the end of the Akkadian era or soon after. His first wife Sarah could not conceive, so *she* gave him her maid as a concubine; this happened again with Abraham's grandson Jacob.

Sargon the Great was notable for protecting widows and orphans. Women were usually married to men who were about ten years older, and the Akkadian men were often called up to serve in wars. This means the empire had numerous widows and "orphans" (who usually had a living mother but no father to protect and provide for them). A woman could use her dowry to support herself and her children, but if it were not enough, she could sell herself or her children into slavery, or someone could adopt them. Boys were adopted for free labor in the fields, and girls could be adopted as household maids or became prostitutes. Cult prostitutes were associated with the goddess Inanna's temples, and some scholars believe Sargon's mother was a cult prostitute.

---

[42] Stol, "Women in Mesopotamia," 125.

This sculpture is of a young woman of Umma in the Akkadian era.
https://commons.wikimedia.org/wiki/File:Female_statuette_Empire_d%27Ak
kad_Louvre_-1.jpg

How did the people of the empire dress? Most clothing was made of linen or wool. Two female sculptures from Ashur and Umma dating to the Akkadian era show young women with wavy hair combed back into a chignon at the nape of the neck and a decorative band around the head—they were simple yet elegant. The Umma woman's high-necked gown falls in layers, with each tier being about three inches. This seemed to be a Mesopotamian fashion trend for both men and women. Several Akkadian-era depictions of the goddess Inanna show her in a short-sleeved, square-necked gown that falls in layers to her ankles; sometimes, a slit on the side of the dress exposes her leg from the thigh down.

Artwork of the time shows men with long beards, which are usually elaborately braided or curled. They have long hair pulled back into a bun and sometimes wear a helmet or cap. The men are often bare-chested (because of the hot Mesopotamian climate) but sometimes wear a coat open in the front or a cape over one shoulder. They wear a simple A-line skirt to the knees or ankles. Naram-Sin's sculpture on his victory stele (see Chapter 5) portrays him wearing a helmet with horns (signifying god-likeness), a long beard, his sword on his back in a baldric (belt) that crosses his chest, and a loincloth that exposes his thighs but drops below his knees in the front and back. His bare-chested soldiers wear simple helmets and a knee-length skirt with a diagonal hemline. Shoes with turned-up toes appear in artwork beginning in Sargon's time. Male prisoners of war are pictured nude in several victory steles.

This diorite statue of an Akkadian man features a long, curled beard, bare chest, and a simple, long A-line skirt.

https://upload.wikimedia.org/wikipedia/commons/4/44/Diorite_Male_Statue%2C_found_in_Assur_%28next_to_the_Anu-Adad_Temple%29%2C_c._2300-2200_BC_%28Akkadian_Period%29.jpg

The environment defined daily life in the Akkadian Empire. The climate was primarily arid or semi-arid in Mesopotamia, with mountains, foothills, grassy steppes in the north and deserts and vast marshy regions in the southern river delta. Akkad and Sumer were extremely hot in the summer, with temperatures as high as 120°F and annual rainfall no more than ten inches, which mainly happened in the winter. The Tigris and Euphrates regularly flooded between April to June, so the Akkadians and Sumerians had hydraulic systems like dikes to regulate flooding.

Clay was an essential natural resource in Akkad and throughout Mesopotamia. It formed the slabs for the earliest form of writing. It was also the primary material for building houses. Clay was readily available in the semi-arid land plains fed by the Euphrates and Tigris, and adobe or mud-brick houses date back to the Neolithic age in Mesopotamia. Trees were not as common, so builders usually only used wood for framing roofs or doors.

Most homes for ordinary people had one to three rooms with a courtyard for cooking and other activities. The roofs were flat and often covered with grain, fruit, or fish, which were spread out to dry. People also enjoyed sitting on their roofs in the evening breeze and even sleeping on the rooftop. Middle-class and upper-class people had larger homes centered around a courtyard.

Generally, builders used sun-dried bricks for the homes, which suffered damage from the winter rains, so they had to slab new clay layers over the houses on occasion. Palaces or temples were built from kiln-dried brick or stone (which usually had to be imported, except in northern Mesopotamia, which had gypsum). The people threw their garbage into the streets; after a while, it would mix with the sand to form a layer higher than the home thresholds, allowing rain and sewage to seep into the houses. Occasionally, the floors needed to be raised above street level.

A natural resource was bitumen, which seeped up from beds in the ground near the Euphrates. Bitumen was a black, sticky substance—something like tar—used to stick bricks together or as a waterproof covering on roofs or other objects. In Sargon's birth legend, his mother sealed his basket with bitumen before floating it down the river (as the biblical Moses's mother did).

In Akkad (and the rest of Mesopotamia), the diet was similar to today's Middle Eastern diet. They grew the native einkorn wheat, which they ground into flour and used to bake bread in clay ovens comparable to today's Middle Eastern tannour ovens. The ovens were usually in the courtyard or a central spot shared with several other neighbors. The dough was leavened or unleavened, pushed flat, and then pressed onto the inside wall of the oven to bake. It was similar to today's naan, lavash, or pita bread. The soil in Mesopotamia grew increasingly saline over time, so many areas switched from growing wheat to barley, which could tolerate the saline soil better. They used barley for bread, porridge, and a thick beer, the latter of which was consumed daily and often drunk with a straw.

They grew legumes, including chickpeas and lentils. They might have lamb or pork that would be roasted or cooked in a clay pot with seasonal vegetables on festive days. They grew fruit and vegetables like garlic, leeks, onions, cumin, cucumbers, apricots, dates, figs, grapes, melons, pomegranates, and eggplants. The Akkadians consumed eggs and meat from waterfowl and roasted or dried fish. They ate a lot of fish! They drank goat milk and made yogurt, cheese, butter, and ghee. When they weren't enduring a horrific drought, the Akkadian diet was high in protein with a wide variety of healthy produce.

The Akkadians' occupations influenced their social hierarchy. They had a five-tiered class system. At the top were the nobility: the king, his governors, and other political leaders. Many governors or others in higher administration were from the king's family. Akkadian governors were the chief administrators in the conquered territories stretching from the Mediterranean Sea to the Persian Gulf, with the Akkadian military ensuring compliance.

The second layer was the priests and priestesses, who were also often members of the royal family. The priestly caste—both men and women—usually knew how to read and write in the cuneiform script. Not only did they organize worship in the temples, but they also served as doctors and dentists in the temple courtyards. Some were astrologists, observing the movement of stars, planets, and celestial changes to predict the future and decipher omens. Sargon established a library with what may have been the first collection of astrological studies.

The upper-class citizens made up the third social stratum. These were the accountants, affluent merchants, architects, army officers, scribes, and teachers. Many people in this class were literate, as reading and writing were necessary for their trade. Otherwise, they had to hire a scribe. It took nine years to train a scribe to read and write cuneiform. The empire had schools to teach reading and writing for the middle and upper classes, and some wealthy families hired tutors.

The fourth social stratum encompassed the lower classes, who were fundamental to the empire's growth. These were the farmers, herders, and fishermen, and they labored to feed the enormous population. Mesopotamia's two most important natural resources were the twin river systems of the Euphrates and Tigris and the annual deposit of silt from these rivers that covered the land during the spring floods. With ample water and natural fertilization, farming or herding was the occupation of at least half of the Akkadian Empire's population.

Some farmers owned their land, usually around fifteen acres. Others were tenant farmers, farming about thirty acres, but they had to turn over up to two-thirds of the crop to landlords and for the "king's portion." Nevertheless, the remaining harvest was sufficient to support a family. The crop portion designated for the king was loaded on barges and shipped to Agade to feed the king's household and his army.[43]

Mesopotamians had been herders of sheep and goats long before settling into cities and growing crops. This time-honored occupation continued to provide wool, milk, and meat; some herders grew wealthy from the sale of wool. Raising donkeys and oxen was also a profitable occupation, as these animals pulled

[43] Foster, *The Age of Agade*, 143-46.

wagons for transport. Oxen also pulled barges up the rivers and canals.

Fishermen and fish farmers provided the most significant source of protein for the empire, as the people consumed astonishing amounts of fish, which we know from delivery documents. They netted fish in the rivers and the Persian Gulf and farmed them in ponds fed by irrigation. Ducks and geese provided eggs, feathers, and meat, and they kept small numbers of pigs for special feasts. Water buffalo appeared on Akkadian era seals and were seen there by traders. They were possibly imported from the Indus Valley.

Other lower classes included basket weavers, construction workers, craftspeople, and enlisted military men who weren't officers. Construction workers for state projects like clearing canals, making or laying bricks, or building roads received food, cooking oil, and wool rations. It was entirely possible in the Akkadian Empire to rise to higher social levels through excellent skills, work ethic, and strategic marital alliances.

Women's employment was usually at home. They ground grain into flour to make bread, wove cloth, sewed garments, tended the children, fetched water from the community well, cut reeds to weave mats, cooked, and cleaned. However, women could acquire land and manage it, which upper-class women commonly did. They also owned taverns. Women didn't have the same high status and legal protection as in the Sumerian culture, but it was higher than in the following Assyrian Empire. The most elevated position for a woman was serving as a high priestess, as Sargon's daughter Enheduanna did. Women priestesses also worked as doctors and dentists, as the medical arts involved religious practices.

The lowest class was the slaves. They were usually prisoners of war, and some were educated or highly skilled craftsmen. A few enslaved people were criminals who had received servitude as a sentence. A man with overwhelming debt could sell his children, his wife, and himself into slavery. Enslaved people were expensive to buy and maintain, so they usually did not do agricultural work. It was cheaper to allot land to tenant farmers who supported themselves and turned over at least half the harvest to the landowner.[44] Most slaves were household servants for wealthy families. Skilled or educated slaves served as accountants, craftspeople, farm administrators, scribes, and teachers.

The Akkadian Empire developed the world's first known postal service, taking advantage of the road system that spanned the empire. The "letters" delivered by postmen in those days were clay tablets with the cuneiform script. The "envelope" began with Sargon's reign; it was an outer layer of clay stamped with the sender's seal. The recipient would crack open the thin outer layer to read the message.

How did a strong empire make trade networks possible? Trade was already well established in Mesopotamia, going back to the Neolithic Age. However, the empire's road system, relative safety, strong alliances, and broader territory ignited prosperous trade with far-flung regions, pouring wealth into Agade and bringing necessary goods and luxury items from distant lands. It also speared astounding developments in mathematical understanding, metallurgy, art, and architecture, as innovations and techniques could be shared and further developed.

Where were the trade networks, and what did they trade? Mesopotamia had a shortage of trees, so they traded with Lebanon for their cedars and the Caucasus Mountains of Turkey for other lumber. Eastern Turkey (Anatolia) was also a rich silver, tin, and copper source. The Akkadian Empire didn't have flat coins, but they used silver "shekels," which were little chunks of silver that weighed about 8.4 grams. These shekels enhanced trade exponentially as an exchange medium.

---

44 Foster, *The Age of Agade*, 149.

The Akkadian Empire's trade routes stretched from the Mediterranean to Anatolia in the north to the Indus Valley in the southeast and around the Persian Gulf.

Map modified: names of seas and regions added. Arrows added to show trade routes. By Middle_East_topographic_map-blank.svg: Sémhur (talk)derivative work: Zunkir (talk) - Middle_East_topographic_map-blank.svg, CC BY-SA 3.0, https://commons.wikimedia.org/w/index.php?curid=17330302

Sargon the Great sent ships to the Indus Valley, trading with the cities of Mohenjo-Daro and Harappa (in today's Pakistan) for cloves, unique shells, carnelian beads, ivory, timber, and cotton textiles. The Akkadian ships also sailed around the Persian Gulf, trading for copper, pearls, semi-precious stones, and linen. The Akkadians traded with Badakhshān (Afghanistan) for lapis lazuli. The Akkadians exported grain, bitumen, woolen textiles, cooking oil, dried fruit, dried fish, leather goods, pottery, and baskets.

Most of the empire's exports were necessary goods like food, while the imports, except for lumber, were luxuries, which points to the astounding wealth of the Akkadian Empire.[45] It had food in abundance (until the great drought), so trade wasn't strictly necessary; rather, it reflected the prestige and social stratification in

[45] Christopher Edens, "Dynamics of Trade in the Ancient Mesopotamian 'World System,'" *American Anthropologist* 94, no. 1 (1992): 122. http://www.jstor.org/stable/680040.

Akkadian society and the empire's esteem and domination over the surrounding areas.

Chapter 7: Warfare and the Military

What was distinctive about the Akkadian military powerhouse? How did this martial force surge ahead to conquer like never before? Sargon the Great said he won thirty-four wars. His core force of 5,400 men was history's first standing army, and this was the first time that military campaigns involved distant regions rather than the neighboring city-states. The newly developed composite bow that used bronze arrowheads was one secret to success, as it was a weaponry revolution.

How did Sargon and other Akkadian kings recruit their soldiers? A principal way was through conquest. Conquered states usually had to do two things: pay tribute (money or goods) to Akkad and provide men for the empire's military. Most empires following the Akkadian Empire employed this conscription method. But Sargon also initiated volunteer corps called *niskum,* who received benefits for enlisting, regular fish and salt rations, and plots of land as a reward when they left service. About one in five soldiers in the Akkadian military were these loyal military professionals.

Sargon organized his full-time military into nine 600-men battalions. Whether volunteer or drafted, the empire's soldiers would soon become experienced in battle since wars of conquest and defense happened most years, along with the ongoing task of crushing sporadic rebellions of conquered states. Sargon also deployed *nim* soldiers; *nim* meant flies in Akkadian. He sent these soldiers ahead of the main body of warriors as skirmishers to harass and distract the enemy like a swarm of flies.[46]

This victory stele celebrates Naram-Sin's conquest of the Lullubi.
https://commons.wikimedia.org/wiki/File:Victory_stele_of_Naram_Sin_9066 .jpg

The Akkadian king was the military's chief commander, and under him were the generals, the top field commanders of the spearmen, ax-bearers, archers, and other units. The Victory Stele of

---

[46] "The Akkadians." *Weapons and Warfare: History and Hardware of Warfare*, 2019. https://weaponsan,dwarfare.com/2019/07/29/the-akkadians/.

Naram-Sin shows him at the top, larger than life, in a horned helmet, facing the conquered Lullubi. One Lullubi soldier in front of him is dying from a spear through his neck. Behind the mortally wounded man, the Lullubi king, Satuni, begs for mercy, and below him, a Lullubi general raises his hand, pleading for himself and his men.

Under the king and his generals were *laputtum* or battalion commanders. The military appeared to use the sexagesimal system (sixties); a battalion was six hundred men, while a platoon was made of sixty men. They were led by a *waklum* or captain. Sargon had a reserve force of trained men in Agade; he mentioned mustering nine contingents from the city. They probably worked regular jobs like our present-day reserves but were trained and ready to deploy at a moment's notice.[47]

Such a large army covering thousands of miles of territory required superior organization for logistics and administration. Since the empire spread from sea to sea and the military continued to grow, Sargon desperately needed capable administrators for his army. He parceled out these bureaucratic tasks to men he trusted. They ensured the soldiers got their daily bread and beer and that supplies and siege engines were transported to the right place. These bureaucrats required a good understanding of the lands through which the military was traveling.

For instance, they needed to know what local water sources were available, how far apart they were, and how much would need to be transported. They knew precisely how long it would take to march from one point in the empire to another. Conquered cities along the way provided food for the army; documents from Umma list the provisions they supplied to the Akkadian military. Scribes traveled with the army, keeping casualty and supply records, accounts

---

[47] "Akkadian Military," *Weapons and Warfare: History and Hardware of Warfare*, 2019. https://weaponsandwarfare.com/2019/09/21/akkadian-military/.

describing their adversaries, and distinctive details of the new lands. A priest accompanied the troops, and he practiced divination to determine the most auspicious tactics. Couriers carried commands and other messages from city to city.

Bas-reliefs and other artwork depict the military's arsenal, including the battle-ax, bow and arrow, javelin, lance, mace, and spear. Various corps carried specific weapons; for instance, there would be an archery platoon for long-distant assault and platoons of spearmen and ax-bearers for closer combat. Spearmen would usually also have an ax, as they would frequently lose their spears after throwing them or impaling someone and not being able to get it back. The soldiers often tucked a slingshot or throwing club (like a boomerang) in their belts.

This rock relief at Darband-i Gawr of Qaradagh Mountain shows Naram-Sin holding a battle-ax in one hand with a bow slung over his shoulder.

On his victory stele, Naram-Sin holds what appears to be a composite bow, which put the Akkadian army at a distinct advantage over its enemies. A simple "self" bow is made from one piece of wood, while a composite bow has several pieces glued together with cattle or ibex horn and animal sinew, providing increased flexibility. The compound bow's velocity was two to three times greater than a simple bow; the arrows could travel at least twice as far and pierce leather armor. Because the lethal composite bow was lighter, it was easier to shoot from horseback or a chariot.

What about armor? Most artwork from the Akkadian Empire era shows no body protection on soldiers except for helmets, sometimes with leather aventails to protect the neck. In the Victory Stele of Rimush, the soldier holding the bow is wearing what appears to be a leather garment. The soldier killing the prisoner has a sash going over his shoulder that is held in place by a belt. If the material were leather, it might have been a sort of armor. Most Akkadian artwork does not show soldiers holding shields, but the Akkadian military probably used "tower shields" like the soldiers of Lagash pictured in the Stele of Vultures.

What tactics did the Akkadian military use? Did they have a cavalry? Did they use chariots in warfare? The Sumerians used a cumbersome four-wheeled chariot pulled by one or two donkeys for centuries before Sargon, and Akkadian art depicts several types of cart vehicles in combat. Scholars initially believed horses did not appear in Mesopotamia until about five hundred years after Sargon the Great based on a lack of Akkadian and Sumerian artwork depicting a person on horseback. However, in 1992, archaeologists unearthed a clay model of a horse at Tell es-Sweyhat (Syria) on the Euphrates River dating to 2300 BCE, which would have been during Sargon's reign. Model chariots found at the same site imply that horses pulled them. Texts found in Ebla indicate that horses were in Mesopotamia even before Sargon's rule. This means the use of cavalry and horse-drawn chariots may have contributed to the Akkadian Empire's unprecedented rise.[48]

---

[48] John Noble Wilford, "Ancient Clay Horse is Found in Syria," *The New York Times*, January 3, 1993. https://www.nytimes.com/1993/01/03/world/ancient-clay-horse-is-found-in-syria.html

The infantrymen (foot soldiers) served in spearmen, archer, and ax-men units. The spearmen could have first deployed ammunition from slingshots before coming close enough to impale their enemies with spears. Cavalry and chariots likely supported the infantry, perhaps launching an initial charge as the two armies drew near each other. If horses and faster chariots were new to Mesopotamia and the Levant, the shock value alone could have sent the enemy packing.

This victory stele, believed to be Rimush's, portrays the massacre of unarmed foes. The soldier on the left is wielding what appears to be a composite bow.

Nevertheless, some fighting wouldn't have lent itself to chariots or cavalry. For instance, the terrain would have been too rough and steep for chariots when the Akkadians fought in the Zagros Mountains against the Gutians, Lullubi, and Elamites. Horses might fare a little better, but the cavalry's advantage was the swift charge, which would have been difficult in hilly, forested battlefields.

Akkadian inscriptions often mention sieges, but they do not include many details of what their siege warfare involved. Sargon mentioned "pulling down" the walls of cities that resisted him but didn't say *how* he got the walls down. We know from textual evidence that Syria used battering rams (*yašibu* in the Akkadian language) in the Akkadian Empire era. Some cylinder seals depict wagons or chariots; some were pulled by horses (or donkeys), and others were propeled by people. A branch of Akkadians settled the city of Nabada in Syria (the archaeological site is Tell Beydar) about a century before Sargon the Great. During the Akkadian Empire, Nabada was an enpire outpost. Cylinder seal impressions from archaeological digs at Tell Beydar show prototypes of siege engines.

One seal impession shows several four-wheeled wagons of different shapes. The vehicle in the top right (and top left) of the scene looks like a four-wheeled chariot drawn by a horse. Two carts appear at the bottom of the picture with no horses. They are both facing a tower-like structure that might represent a tall building (perhaps a city wall). The cart to the left of the elevated structure has three poles extending from it that may be a type of triple battering ram pushed from behind to knock down the structure.

This seal impression from the Akkadian city of Nabada shows what apears to be a wheeled battering ram on the left bottom and a rolling siege tower on the right bottom.

https://commons.wikimedia.org/wiki/File:Beydar-1.png

To the right of the tall structure, another cart with one man in it has a tall front and back wall and is being pushed from behind by another man. This wagon's function is unclear; however, a different picture shows a cart similar to this one with sides almost as high as the walls. They appear to be siege towers on wheels to protect the soldiers and get them up high enough to shoot arrows into the structure. These pictures suggest that the Akkadian military had somewhat sophisticated battering rams and other siege engines.

What were the offensive and defensive strategies of the Akkadian military? The phalanx battle formation was used in Sumer about a century before Sargon the Great, so presumally, the Akkadian army used it. The Stele of Vultures, celebrating the victory of King Eannatum of Lagash over Umma, shows a row of eight soldiers standing shoulder to shoulder with four large shields that cover their bodies from their necks to their ankles. In a typical phalanx formation, each soldier has his own shield, but the carving seems to portray one shield for every two soldiers, which would have been possible with larger shields and double hand grips.

A phalanx formation was used both defensively and offensively. The men held the shields to touch the shields next to them; they might have even slightly overlapped. As long as the soldiers maintained intense discipline and held steady, the phalanx presented a nearly impenetrable wall of defense. The only body parts exposed were the helmeted heads and necks and the feet.

But the phalanx was also a formidable offensive tool. A typical phalanx wasn't just one row of soldiers but multipl rows, one behind the other. The rows of soldiers with shields would march steadily toward the enemy, holding pristine ranks. Meanwhile, archers shot arrows with their compound bows up in th air, over the heads of the Akkadian soldiers and into the enemy raks. With a hail of arrows coming down on them, the enemy would begin to break rank while the phalanx steadily marched toward then

The section from the Stele of Vultures shows a phalanx formation.

Once the phalanx was about thirty to fifty feet away, the soldiers would suddenly launch into a run, slamming into the enemy with their shields. The soldiers in the second, third, and other rows would push the soldiers in front of them with their shields, so it was like a giant human bulldozer plowing through the enemy ranks. In the Stele of Vultures, fallen soldiers lie at the soldiers' feet, crushed by the onslaught of shields.

Sometimes, a tight, strong phalanx could succeed in pushing through the enemy ranks. Usually, the phalanx eventually broke apart, perhaps when tripping over the bodies of the men under them or when the opposing side also had a tight phalanx. When the phalanx crumbled, the soldiers grabbed their battle-axes and maces for hand-to-hand combat. The phalanx formation worked great on a reasonably flat battlefield without trees or other obstructions in the way. But when fighting in the mountains or forested terrain, they had to implement alternate strategies. They would use smaller, rounder shields and engage more with their axes and spears.

Several steles depict naked defeated troops. Some are in chains, which means they probably faced enslavement, while others are impaled with spears or smashed over the head with an ax or mace. When they overcame the enemy, the Akkadian soldiers stripped them of their weapons and clothing. The Akkadians piled the dead enemy soldiers—sometimes in the thousands—in a large mound covered with earth. This hill of dead soldiers might have a monument stele erected at the top, celebrating the victory and posing a grim warning to other cities who might resist the Akkadian war machine.

The Akkadian king needed to be a great warrior to win his people's respect as a leader. Sargon set the standard that others had to follow. He conquered massive swathes of territories, brought in astonishing amounts of plunder, and opened new trade routes that led to unimagined wealth for Akkad. The ideal Akkadian king was fearlessly eager to leap into violent conflict to enlarge the empire's borders, protect his people against invasion, and subdue insurrections.

This concept incurred a paradigm shift in theology. Formerly, the Sumerians felt dependent on the gods for success in battle. It wasn't their fault if they lost—the gods had ordained triumph for the other side. However, especially with Naram-Sin, we see him taking credit for his victories rather than acknowledging divine intervention. When multiple disasters struck near the end of his reign, which ultimately led to the empire's downfall in the rules of his successors, the Mesopotamians latched onto the idea that his lack of piety brought a curse on Agade.

Sargon created the world's first multi-national empire with the world's first permanent army. What did that standing army do when they weren't invading new lands? The Akkadian military was often engaged in safeguarding the domains that had already been captured from internal insurrections and external invasions. Insurrections were met with the mass slaughter of populations and the flattening of cities, even Akkadian cities. The Akkadian military fiercely fought the Gutians, Elamites, and other invaders, annihilating their prisoners or enslaving them.

The full-time military also ensured peace and stability throughout the empire. Battalions were posted in the conquered provinces, discouraging rebellions and keeping the trade routes safe. This relative security led to a surge in trade, enriching the whole empire. Law and order empowered the construction of an empire-wide road system, postal system, the exciting interchange of scientific and artistic developments, and irrigation and construction advancements.

The Akkadians dealt with conflicts and wars differently than their Sumerian neighbors. Sargon and his successors had to adjust to ruling people with diverse cultures and languages. Although he generally left the indigenous religious and cultural practices in place, Sargon found that a "soft" approach was inadequate. He resorted to placing garrisons manned with Akkadian soldiers and Akkadian governors in the conquered lands.

When Akkadian garrisons and governors failed to keep a city-state in line—particularly in Sumer—Sargon and his descendants (especially Rimush) killed, enslaved, or exiled almost entire populations and resettled the land with Akkadians. The Sumerians considered this sacrilege against the gods. Once again, the Akkadian theology conflicted with the Sumerian beliefs that a patron god owned and protected each city and that kingship descended from heaven.

The Akkadians were more humanistic, believing that people owned the land and ruled the cities and that men, not the gods, determined kingship.[49] Of course, the Akkadians were religious and believed they were guided and helped by the gods; in fact, these were the same gods as the Sumerians. They certainly consulted

---

[49] "Akkadian Military," *Weapons and Warfare.*

omens at every turn, but they didn't think everything was owned or ordained by the gods.

The military played a crucial role in the success of the Akkadian Empire. The military enabled the Akkadians to unite all of Mesopotamia under one ruler and then extend the empire in all directions. The Akkadians' worldview led to a new theology of war. Competition was an essential value, as it was more important to live by one's wits and make key alliances and clever decisions than to rely on divine intervention.[50]

Sargon believed he had a divine right to conquer. He thought that he was mirroring the heavenly pantheon by bringing all the city-states of Mesopotamia and beyond under one centralized government. He and the Akkadians believed that humans ran the universe. The Akkadians' theology of war was threefold: 1) struggle within the divine realm of the gods, 2) competition between the military forces, which depended on divine favor, and 3) order and balance brought by the human king. The military's chief role was to enable the king to bring order so that the earth's government mirrored the heavens.[51]

---

[50] Foster, *The Age of Agade*, 236.

[51] Michael Cserkits, "The Concept of War in Ancient Mesopotamia: Reshaping Carl von Clausewitz's Trinity," *Expeditions with MCUP*, United States Marine Corps University Press, (2022). https://doi.org/10.36304/ExpwMCUP.2022.01

Chapter 8: Culture and Art

What set Akkadian art and culture apart from other civilizations? Benjamin Foster, Professor of Assyriology and Babylonian Literature at Yale, summarizes Akkadian art as "a brilliant chapter in the development of iconography and technique."[52] The Akkadians took visual art to new heights. They renovated Sumerian structures into their own imposing architectural style and introduced the world's first named author of poetry, hymns, and prayers. The Akkadian civilization's innovative cultural achievements were in league with their awe-inspiring empire-building success.

Akkadian literature is enriching and fascinating, as it deals with themes like human origins, the reasons or lack of reasons for suffering, and the gods' intervention in history. The themes are reminiscent of biblical stories and poetry, mirroring humankind's struggles, frustrations, and questions. The Akkadian textual record encompasses a wide range, including mundane administrative documents, personal letters, legal contracts, recipes, "how-to" guides, mathematical tables, and medicinal prescriptions. But the jewels of Akkadian literature are the sophisticated poems, stories,

---

[52] Foster, *The Age of Agade*, xvi.

and hymns that help us understand the vitality and complexity of Akkadian life.[53]

Naru literature was a Mesopotamian literary genre that emerged toward the end of the Akkadian Empire. They were moralistic tales involving a human hero—usually a king—and his relationship with the gods. Two predominant Naru literature examples are inscriptions written several generations after the empire's end, but they were about events in the Akkadian era: *The Legend of Sargon*, which we will discuss in Chapter 9, and *The Curse of Agade*, which was discussed in Chapter 5. These two stories blend real-life events (such as the great drought and the Gutian invasion) with the authors' interpretation of divine intervention and sometimes fanciful fiction. Naru literature isn't so much factual historical accounts as an attempt to extract meaning from history or pseudo-history.[54]

Another Naru literature example involving an Akkadian king is *The Legend of Cutha*, which featured Naram-Sin, Agade's fourth king. It is a cautionary tale about following the will of the gods rather than relying on one's own power. The story begins with Naram-Sin bemoaning the fate of Uruk's Enmerkar, who suffered the gods' wrath for no real reason, despite his attempts at divination. Naram-Sin then launches into his own story of inexplicable divine wrath brought by a massive army of 360,000 seemingly supernatural warriors suckled by Tiamat, the goddess of chaos. One by one, this diabolical army destroyed civilizations, such as Subartu, Gutium, Elam, Dilmun, and more.

Naram-Sin sent his soldier with a dagger to stab one of the warriors. If blood came out, they were human, but if not, they were fiends from the underworld. The soldier returned to report that

[53] Alan Lenzi, *An Introduction to Akkadian Literature* (University Park: The Pennsylvania State University Press, 2019), 5-6.

[54] Joshua J. Mark, "The Legend of Cutha," *World History Encyclopedia*, 2021. https://www.worldhistory.org/article/1869/the-legend-of-cutha/.

blood came out; they were mortal. Naram-Sin then sacrificed seven lambs, and seven diviners representing seven gods forbade him from going against the army. But Naram-Sin decided to follow his own heart's counsel, saying, "Let me take responsibility for myself!"

In his first year of the military campaign against the hellish army, he sent out 120,000 men, and the entire army died at the enemy's hands. In the second year, he sent 90,000 troops, and the infernal army obliterated every man. He sent out 60,700 warriors in the third year, and no man returned alive. Naram-Sin was distraught and mystified. How could this happen? In deep anguish, he realized he was a shepherd who had failed his people. How could he save his country?

After humbling himself before the gods, Naram-Sin captured twelve men from the abominable army and brought them back to Agade. The gods instructed him to spare these men because the god Enlil had already planned the destruction of these soldiers' city. Naram-Sin realized he needed to exercise self-control, keep himself in check, and allow the gods to act. He learned he could not save his country through his own efforts but only through divine protection.[55]

Another dominant genre of Akkadian literature is religious poetry, which was written by Sargon's daughter. Sargon strategically placed his children and other relatives in key administrative positions in Akkad and its conquered territories. He appointed his daughter Enheduanna to Ur as the high priestess of the moon god Nanna. Her royal presence would help create stability in southern Sumer. Enheduanna was a prolific writer of hymns and petitionary prayers. She is history's first literary author for whom we have a name. Enheduanna's poetry helped syncretize the Sumerian concept of deities with Akkadian theology.

---

[55] Mark, "The Legend of Cutha."

Enheduanna's name was Sumerian, and it was probably a priestly title, not her birth name. It literally meant "Chief Priestess, the Ornament of Heaven." In her poem, *Queen of All Cosmic Powers*, she recounts her struggle with the king of Ur, Lugal-Anne-Mundu. He was the same king who united with the kings of Uruk and Kish in a revolt against her nephew, Naram-Sin. Sexually harassed, forced out of her position as high priestess and into exile, and feeling abandoned by Nanna, she pleaded with Nanna's daughter, the goddess Inanna:

"Queen of all cosmic powers, bright light shining from above,

Steadfast woman, arrayed in splendor, beloved of earth and sky...

Yes, I took up my place in the sanctuary dwelling,

I was high priestess, I, Enheduanna.

Though I bore the offering basket, though I chanted the hymns,

A death offering was ready; was I no longer living?

...O Moon-god Suen, is this Lugal-Anne my destiny?

...I am Enheduanna; let me speak to you my prayer,

My tears are flowing like some sweet intoxicant...

I would have you judge the case...

That man has defied the rites decreed by holy heaven

He has robbed An of his very temple!

...He has turned that temple into a house of ill repute!

Forcing his way in, as if he were an equal,

He dared approach me in his lust!

...O precious, precious Queen, beloved of heaven,

Your sublime will prevails; let it be for my restoration!"[56]

Enheduanna received a favorable answer to her prayers and recovered her position as the high priestess. She served over forty years and wrote at least forty-two poems about her feelings of frustration with her circumstances and devotion to Nanna and Inanna. Enheduanna's hymns and other Akkadian poetry were clearly meant for performance, meaning they were either sung or spoken. Although rhyme wasn't used, except accidentally, the meter and rhythmic patterning are pleasant to hear, with groupings of two to four lines and repetition of couplets. The works themselves often have lines like, "I will sing" or call on an audience to "hear."

However, the meter wasn't always predictable. Usually, the poems had four accentual peaks per line, but then they suddenly diverged into a different rhythm of three or five (or even more) peaks. M. L. West, a British linguistic and music scholar, theorized that Akkadian poetry was chanted, perhaps to the accompaniment of a harp or lyre, and the performers had an elastic repertoire of intonations, pauses, and inflections. In this way, the irregular rhythms could become uniform, which he felt would mesmerize the audience.[57]

Akkadian art has various categories, bursting with innovation and energy. Sadly, the ruins of Agade still lie hidden under the sand, and they almost surely will yield a treasure in Akkadian artistic, literary, and architectural themes when discovered. But the few examples of sculptures, monuments, and other artistic achievements recovered from other sites give us insight into the ingenuity and skill of the Akkadian artists.

---

[56] Foster, *Age of Agade*, 331–336.

[57] M. L. West, "Akkadian Poetry: Metre and Performance." *Iraq* 59 (1997): 175–87. https://doi.org/10.2307/4200442.

This cylinder seal of Kalki the Scribe (fourth from the left) shows him with the king's brother and other dignitaries and servants.

One type of delicate art, which was used by scribes and administrators throughout Mesopotamia for centuries before the Akkadian Empire, was cylinder seal impressions. Because these little cylinders were so durable—hundreds have been discovered—they can still be rolled in clay to get a fresh image, giving insight into life at the time. The Akkadians seemed to prefer serpentine rock for their seals, compared to the Sumerian civilization before Sargon and the Ur Third Dynasty after.[58] Although mythological themes often prevailed, such as struggles with mythical creatures and between the gods, the scenes were more naturalistic. The sun god Shamash is frequently depicted, along with other deities, such as Ea (Enki) and Inanna (Ishtar). Human heroes display rippling muscles and thick curly hair.

The scribe Kalki's black and white diorite seal shows a picture of Ubil-Eshtar, who was probably Sargon's brother, in the center of five men. An archer in front and a bearded dignitary look back toward Ubil-Eshtar. With a shaved head and face and holding a tablet, Kalki walks immediately behind Ubil-Eshtar, followed by

---

[58] Foster, *Age of Agade*, 202-205.

another bearded dignitary. Two servants, who are only half as high as the five men, denoting their lower status, carry a net and a stool in the back of the procession. The cuneiform script identifies Ubil-Eshtar as the king's brother and Kalki as his servant.

The Seal of Ibni-Sharrum, a scribe for King Shar-Kali-Sharri, displays men watering buffalo by a flowing stream.
https://commons.wikimedia.org/wiki/File:Impression_of_an_Akkadian_cylin der_seal_with_inscription_The_Divine_Sharkalisharri_Prince_of_Akkad_Ib ni-Sharrum_the_Scribe_his_servant.jpg

Akkadian glyphic art (cylinder seal impressions) is notable for the lifelike depiction of humans and animals, but the Akkadians also developed landscape art to new heights. Sometimes, trees, rocks, streams, and mountains form the entire composition, while other times, they are used as background or to separate scenes of men or animals. In the Seal of Ibni-Sharrum, a rivulet of water forms a border at the bottom, while the water buffaloes contentedly drink from the flowing vases.

The male figures display the typical muscular build and flowing mane of hair common to Akkadian art. They are naked, which often implies slavery, yet their elaborately curled beards and hairstyles indicate they are higher class. The Akkadian artists captured an astonishingly realistic portrayal of muscles, tendons, and bone structure. The idealized perfection of the bodies is reminiscent of the classical Greek sculptures that came about 1,500 years later.

The remnants of Akkadian sculpture that have survived through the past four thousand years show remarkable and surprisingly advanced skills for the Early to Middle Bronze Age. Akkadian artisans formed sculptures from diorite, alabaster, and copper. Metallurgy craftwork thrived in the Akkadian era. Metal was readily available from trade routes, and the kings set up workshops for artisans to ply their trade. Copper was inexpensive and abundant at the time, as it was mined in northern Mesopotamia and shipped in from Oman. Bronze, which is made from copper and tin, was used less often because tin became rarer for unknown reasons.

This exquisitely crafted copper head is an unidentified Akkadian king.

The facial features on a striking copper head, perhaps representing Sargon the Great or Naram-Sin, are breathtakingly realistic, displaying haunting beauty and power. Found in Nineveh, the hollow-cast head was once part of a complete statue, and the hair, which is pulled into a bun, and elaborate beard display the male hairstyle of the day or at least of the elite. Sargon's son Manishtushu dedicated a temple to Ishtar in Nineveh, so he may have installed the head (and the rest of the statue) in the temple. In that case, it would be Manishtushu's image.

Another lifelike copper sculpture is the Bassetki Statue, named after the northern Iraqi village where it was found. The sculpture is the endearing figure of a youth. The top has broken off at his waist, so we can only imagine his face, hair, and torso. He is sitting on a flat surface with his legs bent to the side, with his left knee touching the back of his right ankle. In between his legs is a vessel that probably held a standard.

The Bassetki Statue was stolen from the Iraqi Museum in the 2003 invasion and recovered later that year, hidden in a cesspool.

https://commons.wikimedia.org/wiki/File:Bassetki_statue.jpg

A cuneiform inscription in Old Akkadian at the sculpture's base says it guarded Naram-Sin's palace entrance. It says that the citizens of Agade prayed to the gods to make Naram-Sin their city's patron god and built a temple to him after he overpowered a significant rebellion. The sculpture is notable for its amazingly lifelike portrayals of the human body, once again foreshadowing the classical Greek era by well over a millennium. The inscription about making Naram-Sin a god is what later Mesopotamians believe brought down the curse of Agade.

Akkadian metallurgists produced eating, drinking, or decorative vessels but primarily crafted tools and weapons. Mesopotamia already had a sophisticated knowledge of metalworking with bronze, copper, gold, and silver before the Akkadian Empire's rise, but the Akkadians developed new shapes, such as a footed drinking goblet. The craftsmen also frequently inscribed their names or other information on the metal implements.

Most civilizations would consider stone to be useful but not especially valuable. But the Akkadians prized stone, mainly because Mesopotamia didn't have much of it other than some limestone, sandstone, and basalt in the north. When they invaded other lands like Elam or Anatolia, they would happily haul stones back as war trophies, using them for their palaces, temples, and steles. They rarely used stone for sculptures (other than bas-reliefs), but they favored imported alabaster and diorite when they did. One exquisite example is an alabaster head found in Adab (Bismaya) in southern Mesopotamia, which scholars believe represents a king or governor.

This sculpted alabaster head may represent an Akkadian king or governor, dating to the late Akkadian era or the early Ur III Dynasty.

https://commons.wikimedia.org/wiki/File:Head_alabaster_man_akkadian_(pt).jpg

The Akkadian era is notable for steles commemorating military victories—monuments carved into large sandstone slabs or more precious stones from afar. An Akkadian stele usually had a raised bas-relief sculpture projecting from the stone with cuneiform script describing the victory. Sargon was known for setting these up in the lands he conquered, but wind, sand, vandalism, and time have eroded or covered most of what could have been hundreds of steles of the Akkadian kings. These steles were part of Sargon's propaganda campaign to legitimize his right to rule.[59]

An early Sargon stele shows him wearing a long beard almost to his waist, followed by a servant holding a parasol. Sargon's garment appears to be made of sheep hide held together with a belt and with

<hr />

[59] Lorenzo Nigro, "The Two Steles of Sargon: Iconology and Visual Propaganda at the Beginning of Royal Akkadian Relief," *Iraq* 60 (1998): 85. https://doi.org/10.2307/4200454.

one shoulder exposed. He holds a battle net, symbolizing captured prisoners; a row of prisoners is on the section of stele above Sargon. In the Sumerian Stele of Vultures, a god held the net of prisoners, but now Sargon has it, signifying a theological shift.[60]

Sargon (left) carries a net of captured prisoners on this stele. A man carrying a parasol and dignitaries follow the king.

https://commons.wikimedia.org/wiki/File:Sargon_of_Akkad_and_dignitaries.jpg

Akkadian architecture implemented the Sumerian style with some new twists. The Akkadians continued the Sumerian tradition of a central courtyard surrounded by several rooms in their private homes. Since the Ubaid culture, sun-dried plano-convex bricks with a domed-shaped top—looking somewhat like a loaf of bread—had been used in construction. Akkadian builders instead used rectangular, flat-topped bricks of varying sizes.

Administrative buildings and temples were far more imposing; they were made on a grander scale and had thick walls and marked symmetry. The Akkadians built new structures and renovated older buildings to reflect the formidable, colossal style they preferred. A stunning example was the Abu Temple in Eshnunna—a city in central Mesopotamia—which is close to one potential location of Agade.

---

[60] Foster, *The Age of Agade*, 195.

The original small shrine to the god Abu dated to around 3100 BCE. It was rebuilt into a rectangular shape and rebuilt again into a square courtyard surrounded by several rectangular structures. A horde of statuettes depicting worshipers was unearthed from this period. Finally, the Akkadians rebuilt the shrine into one massive form, known as the "Single Shrine Temple." This structure was in a long rectangular shape with walls three times as thick and twice as tall as the one it replaced. It featured a single grand entrance at one end, a platform for cult deities at the other end, and a small nook to one side with a basin for ablutions.

Naram-Sin's son Shar-Kali-Sharri oversaw the reconstruction of Ekur, Enlil's temple in the sacred city of Nippur. The temple has not survived, although later rulers rebuilt it, but records of the builders and materials have. A staggering amount of precious metal adorned the temple—tons of copper and over a thousand pounds of gold, silver, and bronze. Hundreds of craftsmen—carpenters, engravers, goldsmiths, sculptors, and woodworkers—produced exquisite ornamentation: gold-plated bison, copper and gold dragons, gold-plated statues of kings, and many more enchanting works of art.[61]

Akkadian art reflected the empire's power and ideology. The Akkadian kings' patronage of artistic workshops in metals, stones, and other elements encouraged creative brilliance. The Akkadian artists led Mesopotamia into a new era of realistic, lifelike art. Although Akkadian art and architecture reflected Sumerian influence, it was also a type of propaganda to communicate power and dominance. Thus, architecture tended to be formidable and large, and scenes of the kings represented their ascendency.

---

[61] Foster, *The Age of Agade*, 14-16.

Chapter 9: Famous Rulers

We often think of the first four Akkadian kings as brilliant military men who invaded and conquered numerous kingdoms and squelched insurrections. But when these men weren't on military campaigns, what did they accomplish? Which leadership qualities did they display? What were their strengths and weaknesses?

What do we know about Sargon other than his conquests? Is *The Legend of Sargon* simply a fictional account of the man from nowhere? Examining Sargon's extraordinary life, his military exploits, and the Akkadian Empire's founding is like trying to put pieces of a puzzle together only to discover they come from multiple boxes! Accounts tend to be unclear and unreliable. We have a so-called autobiography, but even if Sargon wrote it himself, this man was obsessed with establishing his identity and legitimacy.

Sargon was consumed with proving his right to rule. He had no royal lineage or at least none that he could prove. His parents were obscure. He was called the gardener's son in the *Sumerian King List*, but he said he never knew his biological father in his supposed autobiography. His mother may have been a priestess of the goddess Inanna, but she abandoned him to the river. He grew up in humble circumstances, then suddenly received the honorable position of the king's cupbearer. Within weeks, out of self-preservation, he ejected the king and usurped his throne.

Sargon forcefully asserted his right to kingship, not by his parentage but by the patronage of the gods. In Sumer, he claimed the goddess Inanna's favor and the god Enlil's support. Enlil was a part of the Sumerian triad of chief gods, believed to bestow kingship on whom he chose. A king was not legitimate without his approval. Kings would travel to his temple in Nippur to seek legitimacy, and he would bring lavish offerings. After conquering the cities of Sumer, Sargon wrote this inscription:

> "Sargon, king of Agade, emissary for Ishtar, king of the world, attendant of Anu, lord of the land, governor for Enlil, was victorious over Uruk in battle and conquered fifty governors with the mace of Ilaba and the city of and destroyed its walls and captured Lugal-zage-si, king of Uruk, and brought him to the gate of Enlil in a neck stock.
>
> Sargon, king of Agade, was victorious over Ur in battle, conquered the city and destroyed its walls.
>
> He conquered Eninmar and destroyed its walls and conquered its land and Lagash all the way to the sea. He washed his weapons in the sea.
>
> He was victorious over Umma in battle and conquered the city and destroyed its walls.
>
> Enlil gave no rival to Sargon, king of the land. Enlil indeed gave him the Upper and Lower Sea."
>
> – *Inscription of Sargon*, Old Babylonian copy from Nippur[62]

By washing his weapons in the sea, Sargon symbolized his supremacy over the "Lower Sea," the Persian Gulf. The "Upper Sea" was the Mediterranean. Sargon boasted of thirty-four

---

[62] Foster, *Age of Agade*, 321-22.

successful military campaigns in his numerous inscriptions. A helpful document describing his rule's extent is *The Sargon Geography*, probably written by a Babylonian scribe in the 1ˢᵗ millennium BCE based on texts from the 3ʳᵈ millennium. It seems to be a compilation from various ancient texts, as the author gives accounts that don't always agree.

The Sargon Geography reveals a different side of Sargon—a systematic and orderly man, carefully calculating the measurements of the conquered territories and defining their borders. For instance, he documented one land's borders as extending from "the bridge of Baza on the edge of the road to the land Meluhha to the mountain of cedar: the Hanaean land." *The Sargon Geography* gives two locations for the land of Akkad.

1. "From Hizzat to Abul-Adad: the land Akkad."
2. "From Damru to Sippar: the land Akkad."[63]

Apparently, these two named locations of the land Akkad with different landmarks for its borders came from two original documents quoted by the author/editor of *The Sargon Geography*. Hizzat's location is unknown. Abul-Adad, or "Gate to Adad," was the name of one of Babylon's city gates (Adad was a Mesopotamian deity). We know where Sippar was—on the Euphrates in central Mesopotamia, north of Babylon and Kish, and near modern-day Baghdad. Damru's location is a mystery. But we seem to have two points defining what might be the western border of the land of Akkad (which would include the city of Agade).

---

[63] A. K. Grayson, "The Empire of Sargon of Akkad," *Archiv Für Orientforschung* 25 (1974): 56–64. http://www.jstor.org/stable/41636304.

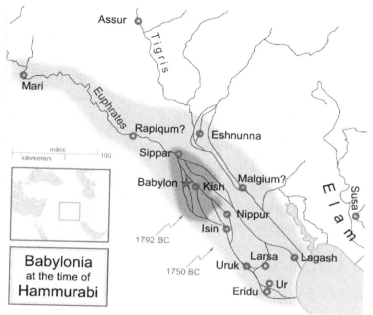

According to The Sargon Geography, *Sippar and Babylon, both on the Euphrates, could be the eastern borders of the region of Akkad.*

https://en.wikipedia.org/wiki/Sippar#/media/File:Hammurabi's_Babylonia_1.svg

Sargon placed Akkadian governors in his conquered lands, and Agade became fabulously rich from trade with all the subjugated territories. It was wealthy enough to feed his standing army of 5,400 men. He ruled a vast empire from the "Upper Sea" (the Mediterranean) to the "Lower Sea" (the Persian Gulf). He erected multiple self-images from Canaan to Syria and decorated his temples and palaces with booty from his conquered lands.

Was Sargon of Akkad the biblical Nimrod? The Torah speaks of Noah's descendent who established dominance over Shinar (Sumer) and then expanded to Ashur in northern Mesopotamia:

> "Cush was the father of Nimrod, who became the first powerful warrior on the earth. He was a mighty hunter before the Lord; that is why it is said, 'Like Nimrod, a

mighty hunter before the Lord.' The first centers of his kingdom were Babylon, Uruk, Akkad, and Kalneh, in the land of Shinar [Sumer]. From that land, he went to Assyria [Ashur], where he built Nineveh, Rehoboth Ir, Calah, and Resen, which is between Nineveh and Calah—which is the great city." (Genesis 10:8-12)

The biblical account does seem to follow the trajectory of Sargon's conquests. He started in northern Sumer (central Mesopotamia), conquering Uruk and establishing or developing the towns of Akkad (Agade) and Babylon into prestigious cities. A tablet dating to Sargon's reign describes him laying the foundations of temples in Babylon. From central Mesopotamia, he continued to expand north into Assyrian territory.

But if he were the son of Cush, the timing wouldn't be right. Cush was Noah's grandson, so he would have lived much earlier. However, Nimrod isn't listed among the five sons of Cush in Genesis 10:7, so Cush must have been Nimrod's "father" in the sense of being his remote ancestor. The name "Nimrod" is not a Hebrew name; it may come from the Babylonian *Namra-uddu,* meaning "star-god." It could even be a pejorative nickname. An alternate meaning of Nimrod (the Hebrew צַיִד or *tsayid*), can carry the meaning of "slaughterer" with a cognate of the northern Syrian Ugaritic word *dbh*.[64] We have no stories of Sargon being a prolific hunter, although he certainly could have been. Naram-Sin spoke of a wild bull hunt. But Sargon was, without doubt, a great slaughterer of men.

Ancient inscriptions on cuneiform tablets provide two parts of Sargon's "autobiography." *The Legend of Sargon* tells how his mother abandoned him to the river, and a man named Akki—an

---

[64] Douglas Petrovich, "Identifying Nimrod of Genesis 10 with Sargon of Akkad by Exegetical and Archaeological Means," *Journal of the Evangelical Theological Society* 56, no. 2 (2013): 273-305. https://www.etsjets.org/files/JETS-PDFs/56/56-2/JETS_56-2_273-305_Petrovich.pdf

irrigator or drawer of water—found him and raised him to be a gardener. Archaeologist Austen Layard discovered two partial copies of this story on three clay tablet fragments in Nineveh in 1867 CE in the Library of Ashurbanipal. Over two decades later, amateur Assyriologist George Smith found a fourth fragment in Nineveh, which helped fill in the second part of the story.

Smith believed these tablets were copies of a much older inscription going back to Sargon's time. However, no tablets of the story have been found dating to the Akkadian period and not even for the millennium following. Of course, Sargon's city of Agade, where such tablets would likely be, is still hidden under the sand. Many scholars believe the legend was written in the days of Sargon II of the Neo-Assyrian Empire, who reigned from 722 to 705 BCE. The Assyrians admired Sargon I of Akkad as an ancient hero and exemplary king; thus, Sargon II took his throne name from the ancient king.

The Sargon birth story (as shared in Chapter 3) says that his mother covered a basket with bitumen, then put the baby Sargon in it and floated him down the river. Scholars often note how this story is echoed later in the birth story of the biblical Moses, whose mother also covered a basket with bitumen and floated him down the river. But which story came first? If the Sargon story was a pseudo-autobiography written during the Neo-Assyrian Empire, the Moses story, recorded in the Torah (Exodus 1 and 2) around 1446 BCE, would predate the Sargon story by centuries.

If the Sargon birth story was written in the Neo-Assyrian era, it would have been close to the time of Rome's founding, which contains another story of a basket in the river. The legend of Rome's founder Romulus says his mother—a Vestal Virgin—gave birth to twins. Her evil uncle, who had usurped her father's throne, ordered his servant to kill the babies. Instead, the servant put Romulus and Remus in a basket, which sailed down the river to be found by a she-wolf. Twenty years later, around 753 BCE, Romulus established Rome.

The Sargon birth story contains several inconsistencies. How would Sargon know his mother was a priestess and put him in a basket? How did he know where he came from other than upstream from wherever Akki the gardener found him? How did he know that his father's brothers "loved the hills?" Unless he was reunited later with his birth family, which could be possible, he would know nothing other than his adoptive father found him in a basket in the river.

In the case of Moses, his sister followed the basket down the river until the Egyptian princess found it. Moses remained in contact with his biological family. Remus and Romulus later met up with their grandfather, put two and two together, and figured out their identity. But Sargon never mentions reuniting with his biological family or how he knew these details. He doesn't even explain why his mother had to give birth in secret and abandon him. If Sargon was the actual author, was he trying to establish legitimacy for an illegitimate birth? His story seems to engender more questions than it answers.

The one element of the story confirmed by the *Sumerian King List* is that his father was a gardener. Several copies of the *Sumerian King List* have survived to the present; at least one tablet's scribe signed and dated it to King Utukhegal of Uruk, placing it around 2125 BCE—less than three decades after the collapse of the Akkadian Empire. Even if *The Legend of Sargon* were a fictional story written over a thousand years later, Sargon definitely scratched his way to the top from humble beginnings. Additionally, *The Legend of Sargon* lines up with the second story, the "Sumerian Sargon Legend," which tells how Sargon rose from gardener to cupbearer to king.

Also known as the Sargon and Ur-Zababa tablet, the "Sumerian Sargon Legend" is a biography of Sargon of Akkad (shared in

Chapter 3). The *Sumerian King List* confirms several story elements. Sargon was the son of a gardener and became a cupbearer to the king. He rose to "kingship" over Sumer by defeating Uruk. The *Weidner Chronicle*, which was written several centuries after the fall of the Akkadian Empire, also mentions Sargon as the cupbearer to King Ur-Zababa. Sargon's monument inscriptions record his interaction with King Lugal-zage-si of Uruk. Other historical records confirm the essential elements of the story.

Two separate manuscripts of the story have been found: a fragment of the story in Uruk and a mostly complete clay tablet from Nippur. Interestingly, the "Sumerian Sargon Legend" is in the Sumerian language, which was dying out by the end of the Akkadian Empire. The use of Sumerian suggests that it was written during or shortly after the Akkadian Empire. Sargon may or may not have floated down the river as a baby in a basket, but he almost surely was promoted from gardener to cupbearer and then usurped the throne of Kish.

What about Sargon's successors? What do we know about their qualities and non-military achievements? Sargon's son Rimush, who succeeded him, seemed exceptionally proud. Rimush called himself "King of the World" even when he knew parts of the world, like Egypt and India, were clearly not in his domain.

Known for his bloodthirsty slaughter of a large swathe of southern Sumer's insurgent population, Rimush diligently recorded the number of people he killed, enslaved, or put into "camps." At that time, tin was a rare metal in Mesopotamia and the surrounding regions. But the prideful Rimush had a statue of himself produced in tin, which he placed in front of the idol to Enlil. He then counted himself among the gods in its inscription. Despite being in the prime of his life, Rimush seemed to decline in the last years of his reign, with few inscriptions lauding his achievements. After nine years, his courtiers cut short his rule by killing him with their cylinder seals.

These fragments from the Victory Stele of Rimush may represent Lagash's defeat.

Although initially passed over for the throne, Manishtushu assumed the reign of the Akkadian Empire after his brother Rimush's assassination. Was Manishtushu involved in his brother's murder? We have no evidence that he was, but he certainly stood to benefit. Manishtushu was an astute military man, further expanding the empire's borders, but he also possessed canny diplomatic skills. These seemed to help him maintain order in Sumer and other conquered lands, as we have no records of the coordinated Sumerian uprisings that disrupted the reigns of his father, brother, and son.

Manishtushu was conscientious about honoring the Sumerian gods, which may have been part of his diplomatic strategy. Throughout Sumer and Akkad, he placed duplicate black diorite statues, which featured him standing with his hands reverently clasped. He especially seemed to target the "home cities" of the most powerful gods, such as Enlil in Nippur and Anu in Uruk. Manishtushu also focused on astral deities associated with the sun, moon, planets, and stars, such as the sun god Shamash in Sippar and the moon god Sin (or Nanna) in Ur. Of course, Inanna (Ishtar), his father Sargon's patron goddess, was highly honored in Agade.

The placement of these statues in key Sumerian cities seemed to be a way of appeasing the citizens after his brother and father had ruthlessly squelched their rebellions and decimated their populations. Manishtushu's figures weren't lauding his achievements so much as honoring the various gods of the cities, declaring his allegiance to them, and acknowledging he only had the power to rule the cities through the blessing of the patron gods.[65] Unfortunately, only fragments of these statues have survived to the present day.

---

[65] Melissa Eppihimer, "Assembling King and State: The Statues of Manishtushu and the Consolidation of Akkadian Kingship." *American Journal of Archaeology* 114, no. 3 (2010): 365–80. http://www.jstor.org/stable/25684286.

This black diorite statue of Manishtushu, missing the upper part of his body, shows him with hands clasped in worship.

By Shonagon - Own work, CC0,
https://commons.wikimedia.org/w/index.php?curid=61159609

After Manishtushu suffered the same fate as his brother—murdered by his courtiers—his son Naram-Sin received the crown. Along with superb military triumphs, Naram-Sin revised and standardized the cuneiform script used to write the Akkadian language. Instead of reading and writing a tablet long-ways, the tablet was turned around, like we read a page today. Spelling was improved, so words were easier to read and write. Even when the Sumerians continued to write in their own language, they used the revised cuneiform script.

Like his father and grandfather, Naram-Sin achieved astounding success in conquering and expanding the empire. However, Naram-

Sin did not seem to possess his father's modesty and diplomacy with conquered territories. This likely led to the Great Revolt he was forced to put down. His success in defeating the Lullubi and other peoples led him to acclaim himself a god. The Sumerians pointed to his pride and lack of piety as the reason for the empire's collapse.

Chapter 10: Myths and Religion

What sort of religion did the Akkadians follow? Like most civilizations, the Akkadian culture included a concept of a world that transcended the tangible earthly, human realm. They had a definite idea of supernatural forces similar to yet distinct from the Sumerian religion. The Akkadian temples, rituals, prayers, and hymns were intrinsic to their lives and reflected their worldview. They were polytheistic, believing in multiple gods, but they thought certain gods were more involved in their lives.

Before the rise of the Akkadian Empire, the Akkadian people lived in Mesopotamia for centuries. Although they had a distinct belief in an all-powerful, supreme, personal god, which was shared with other Semites, they assimilated much of the Sumerian culture. By the time Sargon became king, they were worshiping the Sumerian deities and following their religion, mythology, rites, and cosmology. However, the Akkadians included their own innovations and local variations.

Ancient Mesopotamians believed the supernatural world was comprised of gods and a vast assortment of supra-human ("above" human) beings with powers exceeding human capabilities. These included demons, ghosts, protective spirits, primordial semi-divine sages, and witches. Humans could communicate with these supra-human beings through ritual speeches. Both the gods and the supra-human beings could be benevolent or malevolent to humans.[66] Usually, the same deity or supra-human being could be a combination of kindness and cruelty—even toward the same human! We see this markedly in the prayers to the goddess Inanna and in stories about her.

This gold-plated figurine from the Late Bronze Age represents El (Il), the Semitic supreme creator god.
https://commons.wikimedia.org/wiki/File:El,_the_Canaanite_creator_deity,_Megiddo,_Stratum_VII,_Late_Bronze_II,_1400-1200_BC,_bronze_with_gold_leaf_-_Oriental_Institute_Museum,_University_of_Chicago_-_DSC07734.JPG

---

[66] Alan Lenzi, ed., *Reading Akkadian Prayers and Hymns: An Introduction*, (Atlanta: Society of Biblical Literature, 2011), 9-10.

While the Sumerians and Akkadians worshiped many of the same gods, sometimes their concepts of individual gods differed. The Akkadians also had several gods that were not worshiped in Sumer. One example is "Il," "El," or "Ilum," the supreme god of the northern Mesopotamian Semitic people with whom one could have a personal relationship. The Semites believed Il lived in heaven, but the Sumerians believed heaven itself was the god An, who was distant and remote and had to be approached via another god. The Akkadians syncretized Ilum and An into one god—Anum (or Anu)—and made him the head of their pantheon.[67]

The Akkadian polytheistic concept was that there were thousands upon thousands of gods, just like there were thousands of humans, and each one was different. Some were ranked higher than others, and they all had specific duties. The Akkadians were flexible with their gods, as they readily accepted new ones from the Sumerians or other civilizations into their pantheon.

The Akkadians had three primary gods of the sky. Shamash (Sumerian Utu), the sun god, was the all-seeing, undeceivable judge. His brother Sin (Sumerian Nanna), the moon god, was a mysterious god of divination and decisions. The Akkadians introduced the gruesome practice of cutting open lambs and other sacrificial animals to read the omens Sin had written on their entrails to Mesopotamia. Sargon installed his daughter Enheduanna as a high priestess of Sin (Nanna to the Sumerians) in Ur. The Akkadians' third sky deity was Ishtar, goddess of the morning and evening star who blended into the Sumerian goddess Inanna. She was the goddess of war but also the goddess of familial love.

---

[67] Foster, *The Age of Agade*, 135-138.

Shamash, the sun god, was a chief deity for both the Sumerians and Akkadians. In Akkadian art, size denoted status. Gods were often pictured several times larger than men, kings were larger than their dignitaries, and servants were about half the size of their masters.

The mother goddess of the Akkadians and Sumerians was Mama or Mami, and she watched over childbirth and healed sickness. Ea (the Sumerian Enki) was the freshwater god, an important deity in a land that was mostly desert or semi-arid terrain. Ea was the problem-solving god, and in all Mesopotamian cultures, he was the god that saved humans from the gods' wrath during the Great Flood. Addu or Adad (Sumerian Iškur) was the storm god; in his benevolent state, he brought life-giving rain. In his malevolent persona, he brought fierce storms and floods.

Some gods introduced by the Akkadians and northern Mesopotamians that were not part of the Sumerian pantheon included Bel and Dagan (Dagon). A deity named Ilaba seemed to be specific to Agade and faded away after the end of the Akkadian Empire. The Akkadian word *Bēlu* or Bel and the northwestern

Semitic *Baal* all meant "Lord" and didn't necessarily refer to the same deity. The Babylonians used Bel as a title for their city's patron god Marduk. The Canaanites worshiped Baal as the god of rain and fertility, and the Phoenicians associated Baal with El (Ilum) or Dagan. Dagan was the Syrian father of gods, the lord of the land and prosperity. Like the Sumerian Enlil, he granted kingship; thus, Sargon bowed to him before campaigning in the Levant (Syria, Lebanon, and Canaan).

Sargon established the worship of Ilaba, "god of the fathers," god of war, and Ishtar's husband (at least one of them). A major god for the Akkadians, Ilaba carried a mace he received from Enlil. According to an inscription of Sargon's, "The god Ilaba, mighty one of the gods—the god Enlil gave to him his weapon." Another inscription referred to Ilaba as Sargon's "personal god." What was a personal god? This god was important in a person's daily life, as they took care of the person. If someone's personal god abandoned them, they were subject to dreadful calamities. A personal god accompanied a person into the afterlife, and a Rimush inscription prescribed a curse of *not* standing before one's personal god after death.[68]

Ilaba appeared to be a family god for the Sargonic dynasty, one that was passed down from father to son. One interpretation of his name is a combination of *Il* or *Ilum* (the Semitic supreme god) with *abum* (father), making him the "god of the fathers" or an ancestral god. All of Sargon's descendants mentioned Ilaba in their inscriptions. After defeating a region along the Euphrates River, Naram-Sin gave credit to Dagan for the victory yet mandated that the conquered people worship "his god," Ilaba. Naram-Sin seemed to be setting the stage for Ilaba's elevation from a family god to part of the Akkadian pantheon of gods. His son Shar-Kali-Sharri built a

---

[68] Stefan Nowicki, "Sargon of Akkade and His God: Comments on the Worship of the God of the Father among the Ancient Semites," *Acta Orientalia Academiae Scientiarum Hungaricae* 69, no. 1 (2016): 63–69. http://www.jstor.org/stable/43957458.

temple for Ilaba in Babylon. This was the first mention of Ilaba having a temple, indicating he was now part of the official pantheon.[69]

Akkadian prayers were not all about petitions and requests from the gods. Typically, most prayers—and certainly the hymns—were more about praising the deities, listing their benevolent actions, and speaking about their character and power. This worshipful praise taking precedence in prayer was social protocol for an inferior coming into the presence of a superior. Even petitioning prayers started with abject worship, with the petition usually tacked on at the very end in just one or two lines. However, complaints about a problem might be inserted somewhere in the middle.[70]

Nergal was the husband of Ereshkigal and the god of the underworld.

https://commons.wikimedia.org/wiki/File:Nergal-b.jpg

---

[69] Nowicki, "Sargon of Akkade and His God," 69-71.

[70] Lenzi, *Reading Akkadian Prayers*, 12-13.

This prayer to the god Nergal, who was the god of death and the underworld, is a classic example of a polite invocation and praise of the god. It includes a description of the problem, asks the god to pardon the sin and help with the issue, and promises honor when the god answers favorably:

"Mighty Lord, exalted son of Nunamnir,

foremost among the Anunnakki, lord of battle,

Offspring of Kutushar, the great queen, Nergal,

all-powerful among the gods, beloved of Ninmenna.

You are manifest in the bright heavens; your station is exalted.

You are great in the netherworld; you have no rival.

Together with Ea, your counsel is preeminent in the assembly of the gods.

Together with Sin, you observe everything in the heavens.

Enlil, your father, gave to you the black-headed ones, all living beings, [and]

The herds, the creatures, into your hands he entrusted.

I, so-and-so, son of so-and-so, your servant:

The anger of god and goddess has beset me so that

expenses and losses befall my estate [and]

giving orders but not being heard keep me awake.

Because you are sparing, my lord, I have turned toward your divinity,

Because you are compassionate, I have sought you,

Because you are merciful, I have stood before you,

Because you are favorably inclined, I have looked upon your face.

Favorably look upon me and hear my supplication,

May your furious heart become calm toward me,

Pardon my crime, my sin, and my misdeed,

May the indignation of your great divinity...be appeased for me,

May the offended, angry, and irate god and goddess be reconciled with me.

Then will I declare your wondrous deeds and sing your praise!"[71]

The Akkadians frequently spoke to their gods as if they were family members, calling them father, brother, or forefather. Rather than implore their deities based on their supernatural powers, they spoke to and of them in more human terms, such as "protector," "defender," "wise sage," or "my queen." The Akkadians prayed to their deities about any predicament or problem—even impotency! Interestingly, in prayers regarding sickness or physical problems, the Akkadians referred to their bodies as their "temples," similar to the teachings of Saint Paul in the New Testament.

Mesopotamians had a type of prayer and ritual they called *šà-zi-ga* in Sumerian and *nīš libbi* in Akkadian. It was something like an incantation against evil or sickness; it was not really a prayer to a deity, although they might invoke a supra-human creature. It either asked a benevolent one to help or commanded an evil one to leave. When they pronounced nīš libbi, the Akkadians would say, "šiptu ul yuttun," or "this incantation is not my words," meaning it was some deity speaking through them.[72]

For the Akkadians and the Mesopotamians in general, worship included much more than singing or chanting hymns and prayers.

[71] Lenzi, *Reading Akkadian Prayers*, 339-348.

[72] Lenzi, *Reading Akkadian Prayers*, 14-20.

Body actions were intrinsic, such as kneeling, prostrating oneself face-down on the floor, raising both hands over one's head, clasping hands at the waist or chest level, or holding one's hand in a sort of salute in front of one's face. If in a temple, they would face the cult image or idol. If they were at home or elsewhere in the city, they would turn toward the temple of the god they were praying to; the temples usually towered over the houses and other buildings, so they could be seen from a distance. Worship also included actions such as setting up altars and offering sacrifices.

No recorded Akkadian myths have survived to the present, or at least they have yet to be unearthed.[73] However, a macabre Babylonian creation myth—the *Enuma Elish*—may have dated back to the Akkadian era when Babylon was built. Sargon established Babylon "in front of Akkad," according to the *Weidner Chronicle*. Akkadian inscriptions mention that Shar-Kali-Sharri laid the foundations for Babylonian temples, and one Akkadian document specified Babylon as the border of the land of Akkad. Multiple cuneiform tablets with the *Enuma Elish* exist today, dating to around 1200. However, the scribes who wrote the tablets noted they were copying a story from older tablets that were written centuries earlier. The first part of the myth also parallels the Sumerian flood story, the *Eridu Genesis*.

The story begins before the creation of the heavens and the earth when nothing existed except Apsu (fresh water) and Tiamat (seawater) swirling in chaos. Apsu and Tiamat created the gods by blending their waters. They immediately regretted their creation when the young gods turned out to be annoyingly loud. The youngsters' dancing and playing kept Apsu and Tiamat awake all night. They had no peace.

Apsu and Tiamat met to discuss the situation, and Apsu vowed he would kill the gods so they could have some peace. "No!"

---

[73] Foster, *The Age of Agade*, 211.

Tiamat cried, "We can't kill what we've created!" But Apsu was determined. When the young gods heard their father planned to kill them, their knees gave way, and they collapsed, howling in horror. The god Ea (Enki) was determined to stop his father. He chanted an incantation, put his father into a deep sleep, killed Apsu, and built his house in Apsu's body. Ea's wife gave birth to their son Bel (Marduk for the Babylonians) in their new home. He was a beautiful child with four ears, four eyes, and fire blazing from his mouth.

Bel killed Tiamat and defeated her demons in this bas-relief from Nineveh.
https://en.wikipedia.org/wiki/Tiamat#/media/File:Chaos_Monster_and_Sun_God.png

Tiamat determined to avenge Apsu's death, even though it meant killing her children. Out of the chaos, she formed eleven hideous demons and sent them to massacre her offspring. Ea tried to overcome Tiamat with magic spells, but she was too powerful. The god Anu attempted to appease her but failed. The rest of the gods were too afraid of Tiamat to do anything. But then Bel charged out to confront Tiamat. He blew a cyclone into her mouth, impaled her with his spear, and broke her skull. He then overcame the demons and smashed them under his feet.

Just as his father Ea had made a home from Apsu's body, Bel decided to create one from Tiamat's body. He fileted her body like a fish, and one half became the sky and the other the earth. He appointed all the gods to their roles in the universe. The gods were ecstatic that Apsu and Tiamat were dead and that they were safe. They decided to kill Tiamat's new husband, Qingu, because he had encouraged Tiamat to kill them. The gods created humans from Qingu's blood to grow food and take care of the world so the gods could give their attention to fighting chaos. The gods celebrated their completed work by sitting down to a splendid banquet and passing around mugs of beer.

The Dynasty of Dunnum, also known as the *Harab Myth*, was found in Sippar on a single clay tablet, which was written in the Akkadian language. The tablet itself dates to the Late Babylonian period; however, its colophon (scribe's signature and notes) says it copied collated tablets from Assur and Babylon. The myth recounts the successive generations of gods who gained power by killing their fathers. The patricide is reminiscent of Ea killing his father Apsu in the *Enuma Elish*, except instead of killing their mothers, they married them! The story may have given rise to Sophocles's tragedy *Oedipus Rex* around 429 BCE.

The myth begins with Harab (or Ha'in)—the plow—marrying Earth and creating Sea in the furrows they plowed. This couple gave birth to Sakkan (Sumuqan), the god of four-legged creatures. Earth fell in love with her son and called to him, "Come here! I want to love you!" So, Sakkan killed his father and married his mother. He also married his sister, Sea, who killed their mother, Earth. Then Ewe, Sakkan's son, killed him and married his mother, Sea, who gave birth to River. Ewe also married his sister U-a-a-am. The story continues for several generations of incestual marriages and murdered parents.[74] Imagine attempting to chart a family tree!

This Queen of the Night bas-relief may represent Ereshkigal, the goddess of the underworld.
https://commons.wikimedia.org/wiki/File:British_Museum_Queen_of_the_Night.jpg

A third story is the myth of Nergal and Ereshkigal. Archaeologists first discovered the Akkadian epic myth on a tablet dating to the Middle Babylonian period, but then English archaeologist O. R. Gurney identified it on an Assyrian tablet. Ereshkigal was the queen of the underworld and Ishtar's sister, and she was a Sumerian goddess from ancient times, predating the Akkadian Empire. Nergal was a northern and central Mesopotamian god of the Akkadians, Babylonians, and Assyrians beginning in the Akkadian era.

---

[74] Marten Stol, ed., *The Theology of Dunnum,*

At the beginning of the story, the gods were planning a feast and wanted to welcome their sister Ereshkigal, but the laws of the universe banned her from coming to them, although they could send messages. Anu sent a message to Ereshkigal, inviting her to send her messenger to collect food from the feast and take it down to her. So, her messenger Namtar left the underworld and climbed the stairs to heaven, but, once there, he got angry at the god Nergal. Namtar reported Nergal's offensive behavior to his mistress. Ea ordered Nergal to go to the underworld to apologize but warned him not to receive Ereshkigal's hospitality while there.[75]

Nergal descended to the underworld to apologize, but he fell in love with the beautiful Ereshkigal. He slept with her for seven nights, then returned to heaven. Ereshkigal sent a message to heaven, begging for Nergal to return to her as her husband. However, the gods had transformed Nergal into a hideous creature to disguise him from Namtar, the messenger. When Namtar reported back to Ereshkigal, she figured out what the gods had done, and she threatened to open the gates of the underworld and release the dead spirits to flood the earth if the gods didn't return Nergal to her.

Nergal arrived in the underworld, strode up to Ereshkigal, and grabbed her by the hair. He flung her off her throne; presumedly, this was rough foreplay as a prelude to another extended period of lovemaking. Anu then permitted Nergal to remain as Ereshkigal's husband and king of the underworld. Nergal and Ereshkigal worked out an arrangement where he stayed with her for six months of the year and returned to heaven for the other six months.

Although the Akkadians assimilated the culture and religion of the Sumerians, they also retained some of their earlier gods. The Akkadian theology differed from the Sumerians even when they

---

[75] O. R. Gurney, "The Sultantepe Tablets: VII. The Myth of Nergal and Ereshkigal," *Anatolian Studies* 10 (1960): 105–06. https://doi.org/10.2307/3642431.

worshiped the same gods. The Sumerians believed all fortune and calamity came from the gods; the humanistic Akkadians believed one's actions determined one's life, although the gods could guide them. The Akkadian cosmology gave them "permission" to invade the Sumerian city-states (and other regions) because they believed they reflected heaven's order by bringing all cities together under one central rule.

Conclusion

What were the Akkadian Empire's contributions to ancient history and Mesopotamia's future empires? It was a watershed moment in Mesopotamian history, as civilizations moved from independent city-states to multiple states under a centralized government. Sargon picked up where Lugal-zage-si had started with unifying all of Sumer, then brought all of Mesopotamia under one political system. He continued to conquer large swathes of the known world. Sargon and his descendants set the standard for future empires in Mesopotamia and throughout the ancient world.

Benjamin Foster summarized the impact of the Akkadian Empire as a blend of innovation and maintaining tradition:

> "The Akkadian conquest, therefore, tended to replace community-based government and kinship-based oligarchy with centralized exploitation of resources, despotism, and bureaucracy. To achieve this, Sargon adopted a 'double-edged' policy of both promoting change and selectively linking with the past. He used ancient titles and restored Kish as a long-time center of political power, but founded a new capital at Agade."[76]

---

[76] Foster, *The Age of Agade*, 433.

Consider the colossal impact of just one aspect of culture: the language and writing system. The Sargonic dynasty made Akkadian—the earliest-known Semitic language—the spoken lingua franca of all Mesopotamia and the Levant. A common language united civilizations from the Mediterranean to the Persian Gulf. This unified language sparked a tremendous increase in trade and the interchange of art techniques, military tactics, and scientific and mathematical knowledge. For the following millennia, the Babylonian and Assyrian dialects of the Akkadian language continued as the official languages of the ancient Near East.

The Akkadians also adapted the Sumerian cuneiform script to the Akkadian language, preserving the world's first writing system and spreading a common written language. The bulk of the half-million or more preserved cuneiform tablets are in the Akkadian language (although most are not yet translated). The Akkadian cuneiform writing system continued for two thousand years after the empire collapsed. It was modified by the Babylonian and Assyrians and adapted by the Hittites, Elamites, Hurrians, and other civilizations. It influenced the Old Persian and Ugaritic alphabets.

Another vital contribution of the Akkadians that shaped ancient Mesopotamia and its future empires was assuming control of the temples and their lands. In Sumer, the temples were the most powerful entity, as they controlled the kings, the economy, and the land. The humanistic-leaning Akkadians maintained old temples and built new ones, but the kings now controlled the priesthood, many of whom were royal family members. The government controlled more of the land, distributing some to private owners.

Sargon was the first king to form a standing army. In the past, able-bodied men were called up to fight their neighbors but had to return home for the planting seasons and harvests. The first professional army could fight anytime and anywhere—even a thousand miles from Agade. A full-time army could fight better, having had time to hone weaponry skills and tactics. Sargon and his successors also drafted soldiers from conquered lands. This ethnic mixture of fighting men formed an unprecedented melting pot of cultures—Akkadian, Canaanite, Elamite, Lebanese, Sumerian, and Syrian—all fighting side by side. This military model of a full-time army drawn from all corners of the empire continued through Mesopotamian history.

How did the Akkadian Empire influence our world's civilizations? Danish Assyriologist Aage Westenholz admired the intermingling of the Sumerian and Akkadian cultures, with their equivalent sharing and assimilation between north and south without one civilization blotting out the other.[77] The Akkadian Empire provided a model for future societies to successfully blend cultures, sharing their way of life, ideas, and technologies with others as equals. As cultures learn from each other, they make astounding progress in all aspects of life. Civilizations that welcome cultural blending can adapt, change, and survive.

What is the legacy of the Akkadian Empire? How did its culture, art, and empire-building model endure? The Akkadian art that has survived to the present often features victory steles and bas-reliefs extolling the kings' conquests. For Akkadian royalty, art was used for propaganda, such as celebrating divinely ordained power and expansion.[78] The scenes in the realistic Akkadian reliefs depict a narrative, which goes to show that, since the beginning, art and architecture have been powerfully used to manipulate emotions and deliver an ideological point of view.

Elements of the Akkadian methodology of empire-building have persisted through the millennia in the Babylonian, Assyrian, Roman, Ottoman, French, Spanish, and British Empires—just to

---

[77] Foster, *The Age of Agade*, 443-44.

[78] Lorenzo Nigro, "The Two Steles of Sargon: Iconology and Visual Propaganda at the Beginning of Royal Akkadian Relief," *Iraq* 60 (1998): 85–102. https://doi.org/10.2307/4200454.

name a few. A critical component was bureaucracy. Labor and resources served the kingdom rather than individual people or cities. Enhanced road systems and trade routes provided for easier and safer travel. Taxes supported the bureaucratic administrators, military, and royal family. Scribes maintained meticulous records of accomplishments, taxes, and day-to-day affairs.

What is the legacy of the Akkadian Empire today? Numerous things we take for granted were birthed or developed extensively during the Akkadian era. Examples include a road network connecting Agade to the farthest points of the empire and the efficient water transport on the Euphrates and Tigris Rivers. We can thank the Akkadians for the first postal system, complete with envelopes; fortunately, we now use paper instead of clay! The Akkadians encouraged a common spoken and written language that unified people from diverse cultures, similar to how English, Chinese, and Spanish serve as the lingua francas for millions of people today. Most nations of the world have a professional military—Sargon's innovation—and utilize components of the Akkadian bureaucratic administrative model.

We've really only scratched the surface of the Akkadian Empire's history. Many pieces of the puzzle that would help us fully understand this great civilization and its accomplishments are still missing. More than a quarter-million unearthed Akkadian-language cuneiform tablets need translating. Unrest in the Middle East has stymied the archaeological studies that might reveal new clues. One day, someone will discover the ruins of Agade—how exciting that will be! We can only imagine the treasure troves of historical information that will finally come to light once ancient Agade has been explored.

Here's another book by Enthralling History that you might like

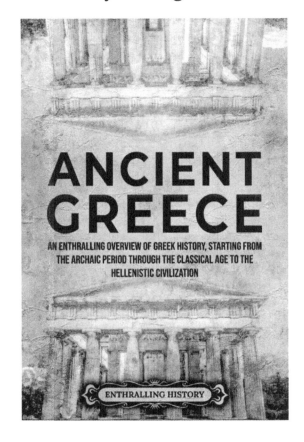

Free limited time bonus

Stop for a moment. We have a free bonus set up for you. The problem is this: we forget 90% of everything that we read after 7 days. Crazy fact, right? Here's the solution: we've created a printable, 1-page pdf summary for this book that you're reading now. All you have to do to get your free pdf summary is to go to the following website: **https://livetolearn.lpages.co/enthrallinghistory/**

Once you do, it will be intuitive. Enjoy, and thank you!

We forget 90% of everything that we've read in 7 days...

Get the free printable pdf summary of the book you've read AND much, much more... shhhh...

Enter Your Most Frequently Used Email to Get Started

DOWNLOAD FREE PDF SUMMARY

© Enthralling History

Bibliography

"Akkadian Military." *Weapons and Warfare: History and Hardware of Warfare.* 2019. https://weaponsandwarfare.com/2019/09/21/akkadian-military

Bertman, Stephen. *Handbook to Life in Ancient Mesopotamia.* Oxford: Oxford University Press, 2005.

Botsforth, George W., ed. "The Reign of Sargon." *A Source-Book of Ancient History.* New

York: Macmillan, 1912, 27-28.

http://www.thelatinlibrary.com/imperialism/readings/sargontablet.html

Carter, R., and Graham Philip, eds. *Beyond the Ubaid: Transformation and Integration in the Late Prehistoric Societies of the Middle East.* Chicago: The Oriental Institute, University of Chicago, 2010.

Chavalas, M. W., ed. *The Ancient Near East: Historical Sources in Translation.* Malden, MA: Blackwell Publishing, 2006.

Clarke, Joanne, Nick Brooks, Edward B. Banning, Miryam Bar-Matthews, Stuart Campbell, Lee Clare, Mauro Cremaschig, et al. "Climatic Changes and Social Transformations in the Near East and

North Africa during the 'Long' Fourth Millennium BC: A Comparative Study of Environmental and Archaeological Evidence." *Quaternary Science Reviews* 136, (2016), 96-121, https://doi.org/10.1016/j.quascirev.2015.10.003

Cooper, Jerrold S. "Sumerian and Akkadian in Sumer and Akkad." *Orientalia* 42 (1973):

239–46. http://www.jstor.org/stable/43079390

Cooper, Jerrold S., and Wolfgang Heimpel. "The Sumerian Sargon Legend." *Journal of the American Oriental Society* 103, no. 1 (1983): 67–82. https://doi.org/10.2307/601860

Cserkits, Michael. "The Concept of War in Ancient Mesopotamia: Reshaping Carl von Clausewitz's Trinity." *Expeditions with MCUP*, United States Marine Corps University Press, 2022. https://doi.org/10.36304/ExpwMCUP.2022.01

Dalley, Stephanie. *Myths from Mesopotamia Creation, the Flood, Gilgamesh, and Others.*

Oxford: Oxford University Press, 2008.

Delougaz, P. "A Short Investigation of the Temple at Al-'Ubaid." *Iraq* 5 (1938): 1–11.

https://doi.org/10.2307/4241617

Edens, Christopher. "Dynamics of Trade in the Ancient Mesopotamian 'World System.'" *American Anthropologist* 94, no. 1 (1992): 118–39. http://www.jstor.org/stable/680040.

Editors. "The World's Oldest Writing." *Archaeology*, May/June 2016.

https://www.archaeology.org/issues/213-features/4326-cuneiform-the-world-s-oldest-writing

Enthralling History. *Ancient Mesopotamia: An Enthralling Overview of Mesopotamian History,*

Starting from Eridu through the Sumerians, Akkadian Empire, Assyrians, Hittites, and

Persians to Alexander the Great. Columbia: Joelan AB, 2022.

Eppihimer, Melissa. "Assembling King and State: The Statues of Manishtushu and the Consolidation of Akkadian Kingship." *American Journal of Archaeology* 114, no. 3 (2010): 365–80. http://www.jstor.org/stable/25684286

Eppihimer, Melissa. *Exemplars of Kingship: Art, Tradition, and the Legacy of the Akkadians.* New York: Oxford University Press, 2019.

Foster, Benjamin R. *The Age of Agade: Inventing Empire in Ancient Mesopotamia.* New

York: Routledge, 2016.

Foster, Benjamin R. *Before the Muses: An Anthology of Akkadian Literature.* Bethesda:

CDL Press, 2018.

"Gilgamesh and Aga: Translation." *The Electronic Text Corpus of Sumerian Literature,* Oxford: Faculty of Oriental Studies, University of Oxford, 2000. https://etcsl.orinst.ox.ac.uk/section1/tr1811.htm

Grayson, A. K. "The Empire of Sargon of Akkad." *Archiv Für Orientforschung* 25 (1974): 56–64. http://www.jstor.org/stable/41636304

Gurney, O. R. "The Sultantepe Tablets: VII. The Myth of Nergal and Ereshkigal." *Anatolian Studies* 10 (1960): 105–31. https://doi.org/10.2307/3642431

Hritz, Carrie, Jennifer Pournelle, Jennifer Smith, and سميثجنيفر. "Revisiting the Sealands: Report of Preliminary Ground Reconnaissance in the Hammar District, Dhi Qar and Basra Governorates, Iraq." *Iraq* 74 (2012): 37–49. http://www.jstor.org/stable/23349778

Jacobsen, Thorkild. "The Assumed Conflict between Sumerians and Semites in Early Mesopotamian History." *Journal of the American Oriental Society* 59, no. 4 (1939): 485–95. https://doi.org/10.2307/594482

Kantor, Helene J. "Landscape in Akkadian Art." *Journal of Near Eastern Studies* 25, no. 3 (1966): 145–52. http://www.jstor.org/stable/543262

King, Leonard W. *A History of Sumer and Akkad: An Account of the Early Races of Babylonia from Prehistoric Times to the Foundation of the Babylonian Monarchy.* New York: Amulet Press, 2015 (first published 1910)

Lawrence, D., A. Palmisano, and M. W. de Gruchy. "Collapse and Continuity: A Multi-proxy Reconstruction of Settlement Organization and Population Trajectories in the Northern Fertile Crescent during the 4.2kya Rapid Climate Change Event. *PLoS One.* 16 (1) (2021). https://pubmed.ncbi.nlm.nih.gov/33428648

Lenzi, Alan. *An Introduction to Akkadian Literature.* University Park: The Pennsylvania State University Press, 2019.

Lenzi, Alan, ed. *Reading Akkadian Prayers and Hymns: An Introduction.* Atlanta: Society of Biblical Literature, 2011.

Levin, Yigal. "Nimrod the Mighty, King of Kish, King of Sumer and Akkad." *Vetus Testamentum* 52, no. 3 (2002): 350–66. http://www.jstor.org/stable/1585058

Lewis, Brian. *The Sargon Legend: A Study of the Akkadian Text and the Tale of the Hero Who was Exposed at Birth.* Philadelphia: American Schools of Oriental Research, 1980.

Lloyd, Seton, Fuad Safar, and Robert J. Braidwood. "Tell Hassuna Excavations by the Iraq Government Directorate General of Antiquities in 1943 and 1944." *Journal of Near Eastern Studies* 4, no. 4 (1945): 255–89. http://www.jstor.org/stable/542914

Luckenbill, D. D. "Akkadian Origins." *The American Journal of Semitic Languages and Literatures* 40, no. 1 (1923): 1–13. http://www.jstor.org/stable/528139

Mark, Joshua J. "The Legend of Cutha." *World History Encyclopedia.* 2021. https://www.worldhistory.org/article/1869/the-legend-of-cutha/.

Moore, A. M. T. "Pottery Kiln Sites at al' Ubaid and Eridu." *Iraq* 64 (2002): 69–77. https://doi.org/10.2307/4200519

Moorey, P. R. S. "The 'Plano-Convex Building' at Kish and Early Mesopotamian Palaces." *Iraq* 26, no. 2 (1964): 83–98. https://doi.org/10.2307/4199767

Nadali, Davide. *Representations of Battering Rams and Siege Towers in Early Bronze Age Glyptic Art.* Universitat Autonoma de Barcelona:39-52. https://ddd.uab.cat/pub/historiae/historiae_a2009n6/historiae_a2009n6p39.pdf

Nemet-Nejat, Karen Rhea. *Daily Life in Ancient Mesopotamia.* Westport, Connecticut: Greenwood Press, 1998.

Nigro, Lorenzo. "The Two Steles of Sargon: Iconology and Visual Propaganda at the Beginning of Royal Akkadian Relief." *Iraq* 60 (1998): 85–102. https://doi.org/10.2307/4200454

Nowicki, Stefan. "Sargon of Akkade and His God: Comments on the Worship of the God of the Father among the Ancient Semites." *Acta Orientalia Academiae Scientiarum Hungaricae* 69, no. 1 (2016): 63–82. http://www.jstor.org/stable/43957458

Petrovich, Douglas. "Identifying Nimrod of Genesis 10 with Sargon of Akkad by Exegetical and Archaeological Means." *Journal of the Evangelical Theological Society* 56, no. 2 (2013): 73–305. https://www.etsjets.org/files/JETS-PDFs/56/56-2/JETS_56-2_273-305_Petrovich.pdf

Powell, Marvin A. "The Sin of Lugalzagesi." *Wiener Zeitschrift Für Die Kunde Des Morgenlandes* 86 (1996): 307–14. http://www.jstor.org/stable/23864744

Rubio, Gonzalo. "On the Alleged 'Pre-Sumerian Substratum.'" *Journal of Cuneiform Studies* 51 (1999): 1–16. https://doi.org/10.2307/1359726

Sackrider, Scott. "The History of Astronomy in Ancient Mesopotamia." *The NEKAAL Observer* 234. https://nekaal.org/observer/ar/ObserverArticle234.pdf

Speiser, E. A. "Some Factors in the Collapse of Akkad." *Journal of the American Oriental Society* 72, no. 3 (1952): 97–101. https://doi.org/10.2307/594938

Stol, Marten. "Women in Mesopotamia." *Journal of the Economic and Social History of the Orient* 38, no. 2 (1995): 123–44. http://www.jstor.org/stable/3632512

Sumerian King List. Translated by Jean-Vincent Scheil, Stephen Langdon, and Thorkild Jacobsen. Livius.

https://www.livius.org/sources/content/anet/266-the-sumerian-king-list/#Translation

Teall, Emily K. "Medicine and Doctoring in Ancient Mesopotamia." *Grand Valley Journal of History* 3:1 (2014), Article 2. https://scholarworks.gvsu.edu/gvjh/vol3/iss1/2

"The Akkadians." *Weapons and Warfare: History and Hardware of Warfare.* 2019. https://weaponsandwarfare.com/2019/07/29/the-akkadians

The Code of Hammurabi. Translated by L.W. King. The Avalon Project: Documents in Law, History, and Diplomacy. Yale Law School: Lillian Goldman Law Library. https://avalon.law.yale.edu/ancient/hamframe.asp

The Curse of Agade. Translated by Jerrold S. Cooper. Baltimore: Johns Hopkins University

Press, 1983.

The Epic of Atrahasis. Translated by B. R. Foster. Livius. https://www.livius.org/sources/content/anet/104-106-the-epic-of-atrahasis

The Epic of Gilgamesh. Academy of Ancient Texts. https://www.ancienttexts.org/library/mesopotamian/gilgamesh

"The Legend of Sargon of Akkadê." *Ancient History Sourcebook.* New York: Fordham University, 1999. https://sourcebooks.fordham.edu/ancient/2300sargon1.asp

"The Sargon Geography." Translated by Wayne Horowitz. *Mesopotamian Cosmic Geography.* Winona Lake: Eisenbrauns 1998

http://www.aakkl.helsinki.fi/melammu/database/gen_html/a0000526.php

The Tummal Chronicle. Livius. https://www.livius.org/sources/content/mesopotamian-chronicles-content/cm-7-tummal-chronicle

Van Buren, E. Douglas. "Discoveries at Eridu." *Orientalia* 18, no. 1 (1949): 123–24. http://www.jstor.org/stable/43072618

Van De Mieroop, Marc. *A History of the Ancient Near East ca. 3000 - 323 BC.* Hoboken: Blackwell Publishing, 2006.

Wall-Romana, Christophe. "An Areal Location of Agade." *Journal of Near Eastern*

Studies 49, no. 3 (1990): 205–45. http://www.jstor.org/stable/546244

Weidner Chronicle (ABC 19). Livius, 2020. https://www.livius.org/sources/content/mesopotamian-chronicles-content/abc-19-weidner-chronicle

Weiss, Harvey. *Megadrought and Collapse.* New York: Oxford University Press, 2017.

Weiss, H., M. A. Courty, W. Wetterstrom, F. Guichard, L. Senior, R. Meadow, and A.

Curnow. "The Genesis and Collapse of Third Millennium North Mesopotamian Civilization." *Science* 261, no. 5124 (1993): 995–1004.

http://www.jstor.org/stable/2881847

West, M. L. "Akkadian Poetry: Metre and Performance." *Iraq* 59 (1997): 175–87.

https://doi.org/10.2307/4200442

Westenholz, Joan Goodnick. "Heroes of Akkad." *Journal of the American Oriental Society*

103, no. 1 (1983): 327–36. https://doi.org/10.2307/601890

Westenholz, Joan Goodnick. *Legends of the Kings of Akkade: The Texts.* Winona Lake:

Eisenbrauns, 1997.

Wilford, John Noble. "Ancient Clay Horse is Found in Syria." *The New York Times,*

January 3, 1993.

https://www.nytimes.com/1993/01/03/world/ancient-clay-horse-is-found-in-syria.html

Wilkinson, T. J., B. H. Monahan, and D. J. Tucker. "Khanijdal East: A Small Ubaid Site in Northern Iraq." *Iraq* 58 (1996): 17–50. https://doi.org/10.2307/4200417

Woolley, C. Leonard. "Excavations at Ur." *Journal of the Royal Society of Arts* 82, no. 4227 (1933): 46–59. http://www.jstor.org/stable/41360003

Ziskind, Jonathan R. "The Sumerian Problem." *The History Teacher* 5, no. 2 (1972): 34–41. https://doi.org/10.2307/491500

Made in the USA
Monee, IL
20 August 2022

12017838R00089